REIGN

THE CHURCH IN THE MIDDLE AGES

LUKE H. DAVIS

CF4·K

10 9 8 7 6 5 4 3 2

Copyright © 2022 Luke H. Davis
Reprinted in 2024
Paperback ISBN: 978-1-5271-0801-1
Ebook ISBN: 978-1-5271-0885-1

Published by Christian Focus Publications,
Geanies House, Fearn, Tain, Ross-shire,
IV20 1TW, Scotland, U.K.
www.christianfocus.com;
email: info@christianfocus.com

Design and illustration: Laura K. Sayers
Cover design: James Amour

Printed and bound in Malaysia

All rights reserved. No part of this publication may be reproduced, stored in a retrieval system, or transmitted, in any form, by any means, electronic, mechanical, photocopying, recording or otherwise without the prior permission of the publisher or a licence permitting restricted copying. In the U.K. such licences are issued by the Copyright Licensing Agency, 4 Battlebridge Lane, London, SE1 2HX. www.cla.co.uk

Scripture quotations are from The Holy Bible, English Standard Version, copyright © 2001 by Crossway Bibles, a publishing ministry of Good News Publishers. Used by permission. All rights reserved. esv Text Edition: 2011.

Luke Davis has written a grand "human" introduction to the Church in the Middle Ages. Focusing on the Western Church, although not ignoring the East, he enables us to encounter many of the leading Christians of the day – Churchmen, dissenters, men, women, theologians, preachers, and mystics. An ideal springboard to propel readers into further study of a sadly neglected period in church history.

Dr Nick Needham,
Highland Theological College, Dingwall, UK

In *Reign; The Church in the Middle Ages*, Luke Davies takes you on a wild and turbulent journey spanning 1,000 years of church history. Luke gives a unique insight into the controversies of the church and how faithful people stood firm in their faith and held the gospel high. This book will teach you, at times you'll laugh and at times you'll be sitting on the edge of your seat wondering what's coming next. This is definitely worth a read!

Alistair Chalmers,
Assistant Pastor, Bruntsfield Evangelical Church, Edinburgh

Luke Davis has done an impressive job of telling the history of medieval Christianity for young adults through a skilful use of story and traditional narrative. He has taken seriously the importance of the thousand years of the Middle Ages that many Evangelicals wrongly write off as a spiritual wasteland. This is a period of time when God was at work, when the church got some things right but also made some big mistakes. The entire era has much to teach us. Highly recommended!

Michael A.G. Haykin,
The Southern Baptist Theological Seminary,
Louisville, Kentucky.

Once a man lived and died in poverty, unaware of the buried treasure beneath his property. Even so, the Christian church today is at risk of forgetting the riches of its own history. It matters little how magnificent the stories may be, if the truth remains buried, or if the records are locked away in archaic or arcane language that people cannot grasp. In *Redemption* and *Reign*, Luke Davis selects pivotal moments from history, to which he applies an imagination like that of a Hollywood filmmaker. The past jumps into razor-sharp focus, as the reader sees, hears, and feels these episodes happening once again. Davis is no narrow sectarian, seeking to exalt some believers at the expense of others, but instead approaches the Christian past with generous orthodoxy, finding lessons to be learned in far-flung times and places. These volumes are an ideal first book for younger readers, and—quite frankly—for some not-so-younger readers too. Whatever a reader's age, Davis's books are a perfect appetizer for those tasting the delights of church history for the first time, who will then be likely to return for a full meal.

Michael J. McClymond, Ph.D.
Professor of Modern Christianity
Department of Theological Studies, Saint Louis University
St. Louis, Missouri, USA

Luke Davis has given the reader a ringside seat to the parade of people who have made a difference in the history of the church. Sorting out heresies within and persecutions without, the church called for courageous men and women who stand for the truth. Those are the people you will find in the pages of this book. So sit back and enjoy, and learn how God used his people to care for and guard his church.

Linda Finlayson
Author of *God's Timeline* and *God's Bible Timeline*

According to the Psalms, God's people praise and glorify Him as they tell of His mighty acts from one generation to the next (Psalm 145:4). Today the church is in need of storytellers who will teach the next generation the great things God has done through His people throughout the centuries. With sparkling prose, backed by solid research, Luke Davis makes church history come alive for the young reader (and readers of all ages!). What makes this work unique is that it offers engaging historical fiction but also provides timelines, factual summaries of significant figures and events, and insightful reflection. This is a powerful combination. You will be inspired to serve the Lord today, as you read of the trials and triumphs of the saints who have gone before us. I look forward to sharing these stories with my children!

Ben Wagner
Rector of Anglican Church of the Resurrection,
Chesterfield, Missouri

CONTENTS

DEDICATED IN MEMORY OF

Dr. Roger Munsick

lover of history,
bastion of good will,
reservoir of steadfast faith

with many thanks
for your grand, gregarious, and glorious friendship

IMPORTANT MOMENTS IN THE ANCIENT CHURCH

476
Roman Empire defeated by the Germans under Odoacer

516
Benedict of Nursia writes his Rule

530
Founding of Monte Cassino monastery

563
Columba leaves Ireland and founds the abbey at Iona, Scotland

590
Pope Gregory I writes his Pastoral Rule

610
Muhammad's vision in a cave; the beginning of Islam

632
Death of Muhammad

711
Invasion of Spain by Moors

732
Battle of Tours, France; Charles Martel defeats Moorish forces

800
Charlemagne crowned Holy Roman Emperor

818
Theodulf of Orleans is deposed as bishop and exiled to Angers

988
Prince Vladimir of Kiev is baptized and Christianizes his kingdom

1054
The Catholic West and Orthodox East divide in the East-West Schism

1093
Anselm is consecrated Archbishop of Canterbury

1099
Crusaders take Jerusalem from Seljuk Turks

1115
Bernard founds the monastery at Clairvaux

1180
Peter Waldo and his followers are expelled from Lyon, France

1209
Pope Innocent III orders a crusade to destroy the Cathars in Albi

1210
Francis of Assisi founds the Order of Friars Minor (Franciscans)

1215
King John signs Magna Carta at Runnymede

1265-74
Thomas Aquinas writes his *Summa Theologica*

1291

Acre falls to Muslim armies, ending the final Crusade

1320

Dante Alighieri completes his *Divine Comedy*

1346-53

The Black Death ravages Europe, killing at least a third of all people

1373

Julian of Norwich recovers from illness, begins writing her *Revelations*

1384

John Wycliffe completes his translation of the entire Bible into English

1415

John Hus is condemned to death at the Council of Constance

1427

Thomas a Kempis finishes writing *The Imitation of Christ*

1485

The Battle of Bosworth Field ends the War of the Roses

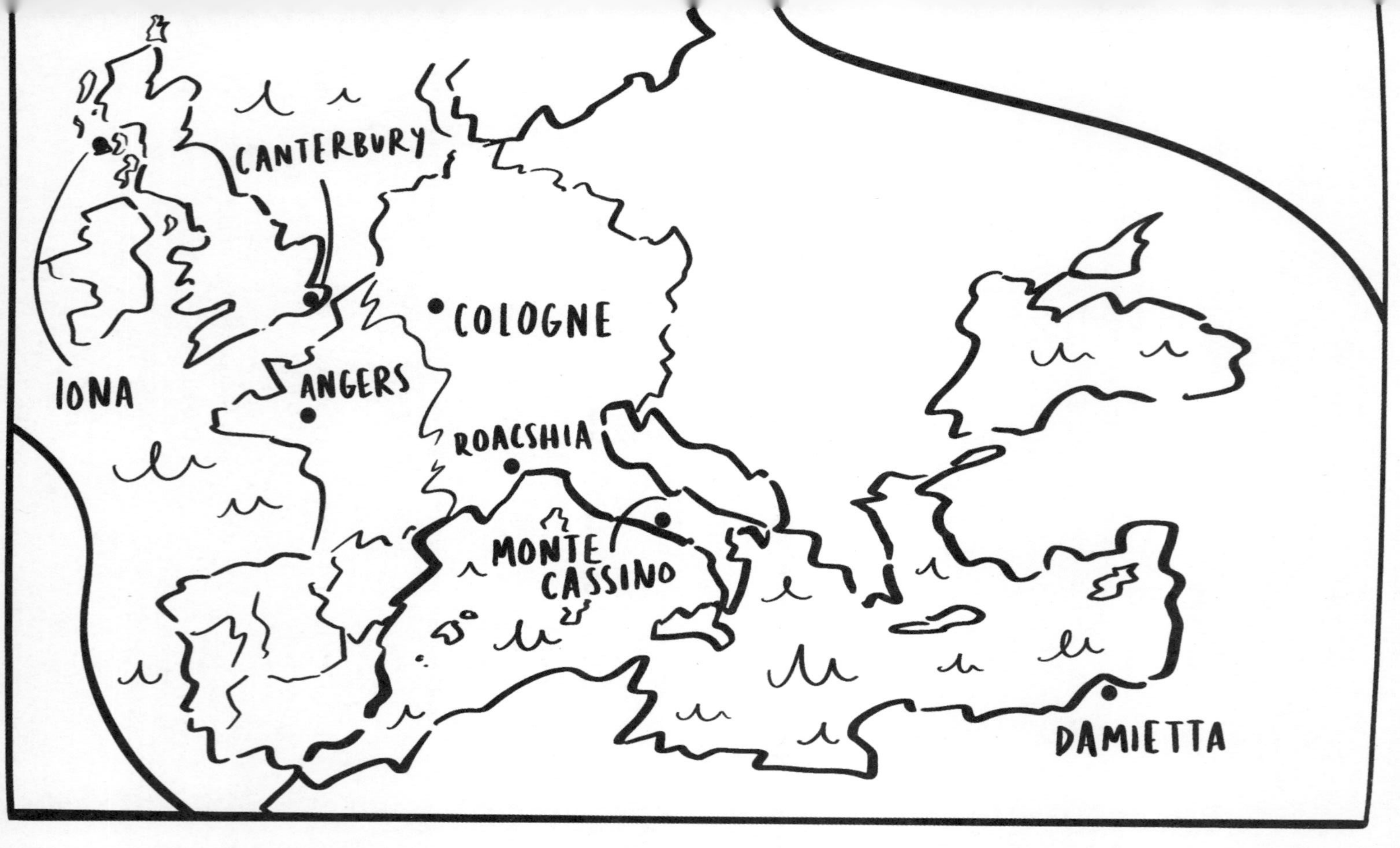
CANTERBURY
IONA
COLOGNE
ANGERS
ROACSHIA
MONTE CASSINO
DAMIETTA

THE MEDIEVAL CHURCH

"The more things change, the more they stay the same." At no point were those words more appropriate than the medieval times between 476 and 1485. The reason we call this era "medieval" is because it comes from Latin words for "middle" and "age", so we often refer to this time as the Middle Ages.

In truth, the Middle Ages were a time of incredible change and upheaval. Through invasions and charges of numerous barbarian tribes, the Roman Empire fractured over the course of the fifth century A.D. Goths, Vandals, and many Germanic tribes flooded the regions once filled with Roman armies that held them at bay. In time, these peoples divided up what was left of the empire, carving kingdoms of the Burgundians, Franks, Visigoths, Ostrogoths, and Lombards out of the western European continent. Groups such as the Scots, Picts, Irish, Angles, and Saxons dwelt in Britain. With Europe divided into smaller kingdoms, trade and commerce collapsed along with the safety of many travel routes. The highly established Roman manner of administration and government fell apart, with each local kingdom maintaining its own particular way of law. Literacy among the masses fell, and it was several years before schools began to be established for the sake of educating citizens. Even agriculture declined as many farmers struggled to maintain quality harvests. Seeking some kind of structure, many kingdoms in medieval Europe adopted a land-based structure of everyday life. Society was layered by classes of kings, nobles, knights, and peasants to tend land and provide for the economic stability of a region.

As the Middle Ages progressed, forceful leaders began to unite kingdoms and provide for the flourishing of those within their borders. Charlemagne was crowned Holy Roman Emperor on Christmas Day 800 in Rome by Pope Leo III in hopes of bringing together a number of regions under one banner. In spite of many positive reforms, Charlemagne and his descendants ruled over a loose federation of peoples. It was not holy, nor Roman, nor an empire. However, as the powers of kings continued to rise, they paralleled the force of strong popes such as Innocent III, often leading to spectacular clashes. The borders of nations began to take shape as kingdoms warred against one another, and then these conflicts quieted somewhat when they combined their armies against the Muslims in the Crusades. Originally a call to free the Holy Land of Israel from the clutch of the Seljuk Turks, the Crusades demonstrated the thirst for power and wealth amongst many knights, who sometimes committed vile sins and atrocious actions on those they conquered.

Paralleling the expansion of the Church's reign over many areas of human existence, monks, theologians, and clergy labored with all their hearts and souls to build a community of faith that was more of a reflection of the spiritual family that God intended. Benedict, Columba, and Francis organized communities in which the Gospel could be demonstrated, lived, and preached to others. When theology and community needed to be transformed in fresh ways, Theodulf, Anselm, and Bernard of Clairvaux answered the call. Gregory the Great reformed worship and the role of bishops. Stephen Langton negotiated arguably the greatest document of human liberty while securing freedom for the Church. The presence of God among His people was rediscovered in varied ways by theologians like Thomas Aquinas and mystics like Julian of Norwich. And when corruption took hold of the Church and leaders drifted from the authority of Scripture, a first wave of reformers in Peter Waldo, John Wycliffe, and John Hus arose to call God's people back to the grace of God offered in the Bible.

In all, the Middle Ages offer an energetic swath of activity and understanding. The Church, since the Council of Nicea in 325, had been taking on more of a shaping role in the life of European society, and this created many versions of the people of God on earth.

We have a Church that sought to reign, a Church that desired to love, a Church that pursued conquest, a Church that wanted to secure freedom, a Church that looked to proclaim the Gospel, a Church that craved the presence of God, a Church that fell into corruption, and a Church that undertook its own reform. Which one of these is the medieval Church? They all are! And in that we can find hope in the God Who loves His Church and humility as we seek to live in His name.

BENEDICT

538, Monte Cassino, Italy

The gates of the great monastery swung open, and trudging in came a score of townspeople, ragged, thin, and worn. Standing his post by the gate, Rodolfino could detect dread in every step of every living soul. This is no quiet anxiety, he mused. This is a horror that they have no energy to express properly.

"Good sir," he called to the first man through, who was holding a small girl in his arms, "do you require shelter? Food? Drink?"

"All of them," the man coughed, placing the child in Rodolfino's hands and collapsing to the ground in a hacking fit. A man and a woman—by the looks of them, Rodolfino thought, his son and daughter—came to each side and steadied him. The son looked up.

"Accept our apologies, good brother" he said, "but we have nowhere to go but here. The lack of food is too great, and with the enemy approaching we cannot remain in harm's way!"

"The enemy?" Rodolfino asked before noticing his fellow gardener passing by. "Quickly!" he said. "Go and fetch the Father! We have guests in severe need. Hurry!" As the other monk scurried off toward the church, Rodolfino turned back to the travelers. "Which enemy do you speak of?"

"The soldiers come to burn our town!" cried a little boy who wrested free from his mother's grip. "They come for us now!"

"Have a care, my son," his mother wept.

"Please," came the voice of a burly fellow with a sword sheathed at his side. Hobbling forward on what was clearly a twisted ankle, he put forth his hand to grip Rodolfino's. "I am the judge of Sant Elia. Forgive our ragged appearance, but we have walked over harsh ground for a day and a half because the Huns and Slavs have certainly fallen upon our village by now."

"The Huns and Slavs?" Rodolfino gasped as several of the women began crying. "They are swarming the hills even now?"

"They are..." began the judge before noticing a cloaked figure approach them from behind Rodolfino. "Benedict! Praise God for you! Oh, Benedict!" And the judge fell to his knees before the abbot, grabbing his hand and kissing it as Benedict stopped, smiling, looking over the gathered masses with warm, shining eyes.

"Rodolfino," Benedict quietly said, "can you and a couple more of the brothers please escort our guests to the refectory and give them what food we have available? I will bring along my friend and we can speak quietly there."

"We will have to stretch our supplies, Father," Rodolfino whispered, almost indistinctly.

"And they are guests in need, Brother Rodolfino," Benedict replied, his hand on the weeping judge's head. "Let us always receive them as we would receive the Lord Jesus Christ."

"The news everywhere is horrifying," the judge explained in the infirmary as a monk cared for his swollen ankle with some cloths soaked in warm water. "Eleven months ago, upwards of sixteen hundred Huns and Slavs came by ship from Constantinople, and then seven months later five thousand more warriors joined them." He winced as his foot was shifted onto a towel.

"The enemy swarmed over the land and took Rome, practically without a fight."

"Why was there such little resistance?" Benedict asked, his eyes showing a flicker of worry but his voice steady and calm. "Didn't King Vitiges head them off?"

"Vitiges is brave but reckless," the judge groaned over the pain. "He won a great victory over his foe Belisarius in open battle, but before long the army ran out of food and supplies. Our allies were surrounded and butchered. Now remnants of the Huns and Slavs are also roaming the countryside all the way to Campania, burning, looting, and doing all manner of unspeakable things." He grunted as the monk finished wrapping his foot.

"That should hold, sire," the monk nodded and stepped back, as if to admire his handiwork. "Walk if you must, but it will be important to rest that foot for as long as you can."

"Might we join the people for some food," the judge asked, "but only after you, Father Benedict, show me this place you have created?"

"God has built this monastery," Benedict answered, "and I have merely moved some stone, wood, and earth for His glory. But it would be my humble honor to show you what God has done."

"This is different from what I hear of the monasteries in the East," the judge marveled. "They brag about the austerity and hardness of their dwellings as if to say that cruelty and misery brings one close to God. Father Benedict, you seem to say otherwise."

"In times of scarcity, we should be content with little, I agree," Benedict said, walking slowly toward a workshop so that his guest could keep up. "But I do not believe God calls us all to extreme difficulty, especially the sort that leads to boasting. When I sat down to write my Rule years ago, the Lord granted me the insight to recognize that what is needed for my fellow monks is not harshness, but ordering their lives and mine wisely with strict discipline, a discipline that flows from a firm conviction of the love of Christ. Yes, the Byzantine monks live on bread, salt, and water, and they may do so. But for us to be about the work of God, we require strength to do so. This is why we have two meals per day. Both are cooked over flame, and we manage to grow and provide our own fruits and vegetables for our meals."

"Is that a wine cellar by the south wall?" asked the judge, pointing.

"Indeed it is," Benedict smiled, "for we have a small amount each day. A content monk is a dutiful servant of Christ. The energy we receive from food and rest strengthens us for our everyday effort. Ora et labora, Theudo. Prayer and work. Those are the cornerstones of our mission here at Monte Cassino. Some monks work in the wine press. Others," he gestured as they approached a carpentry room, "labor here."

"Wood!" his guest said, his eyes wide. "And you have tools and tables upon which to construct these...". He stopped, staring at what lay upon the table. "Is that a headboard with the carving of a dove? It is the same style and carving as the bed I own. However, I bought that at the market shop in Sant Elia!"

Benedict cocked his head and raised his eyebrows. "How do you think it got there?"

"So my bed was made here, by your monks?" he replied, amazed.

"Indeed. Everyone here has the opportunity to serve as a craftsman, a cook, a gardener, a winemaker, a scribe," said Benedict. "Like the Church of Christ, we depend on one another, and we provide for one another's needs." They approached the church at the center of Monte Cassino. "And here is where the center of our life takes place."

"Your prayers are the center?" the judge asked.

"As the Psalmist said, 'Seven times a day, I rise and praise you' and 'At midnight, I rise to praise you'. So, we endeavor to live likewise."

"By prayer as well as your work?"

"Prayer is our work," Benedict replied emphatically. "Physical labor is of great value and keeps our hands from being idle. But we are called to worship and praise our heavenly King. In fact, you have come just as we are approaching our prayer service at the end of the day. We would be most honored for you to join us in the church before taking your rest."

"Father Benedict!" came a strident call from across the yard. Running at a full sprint was Rodolfino, who wore a clearly anguished face.

"Brother Rodolfino, what news?" asked Benedict.

"Our worst fears have been realized, Father," the monk huffed, out of breath. "We have no bread!"

"No bread?" Benedict inquired, disbelieving. "I know food has been scarce, but surely we had more wheat than that."

"Five loaves remain, Father! Tomorrow at breakfast, we will be out of bread!"

"We will have to go to a settlement to the south and buy what we can or trade some wine," Benedict thought aloud.

"That raises the second problem, Father!"

"What is that?"

"A raiding party of Slavs has come from the direction of Sant Elia and is making for the monastery!" Rodolfino blurted out. "They will certainly be here after nightfall if they do not break pace! If some among us go to find food, there might not be a monastery to return to."

Benedict sensed the judge faltering at his side, and instinctively reached out to steady him. "Brother Rodolfino," he calmly spoke, "gather the monks and the guests from the refectory and bring them here to the church."

"Father, did you not hear what I just told you?"

"I did," Benedict replied evenly. "And I would remind you that even as dangers swarm around our family, the hours of prayer still stand firm."

"But Father..."

"Brother Rodolfino, I am not asking you to give weight to your fears, I am reminding you that Christ is our shepherd even in apparent danger. Calm yourself. Gather all the monks. Bring the guests here. And do so immediately."

The evening breezes wafted through the air as forty-five souls huddled inside the church and Benedict moved through the crowd toward the altar. Rodolfino had lit twelve candles, six on each side of the nave, and the flickering lights cast an eerie, inconstant glow throughout the church. Soft murmurs and whimpers of anxiety escaped from the mouths of many in the assembly, but when Benedict reached the front altar and turned to face the congregation, not a sound could be heard. He raised his hands to heaven.

"The Lord Almighty grant us a peaceful night," he began, "and a perfect end."

"Amen," came the reply of the people.

They joined together to confess their sins, asking God for forgiveness, for changed desires, and for the love of God to dwell in their hearts. Benedict cleared his throat and called out, "O God, make speed to save us!"

"O Lord, make haste to help us!"

The words were not a mumble, but an earnest groaning from the hearts of the faithful. The words of the congregation faded as Benedict folded his hands to recite a psalm, when a flurry of noise broke overhead. Looking up, Benedict peered at the small slit of the window behind the altar and saw a black form thrash downward toward him. Putting up his hands for protection, Benedict and the entire congregation gave an awed gasp as a raven perched on the abbot's arm!

For a few seconds, nobody moved or spoke. Then Benedict's face split into a wide grin as he took his opposite hand and stroked the raven's head.

"Hello, little one," he whispered. "Have you come to assure us that we will be protected?"

The raven cocked its head to the side, looked at Benedict, then at the people, and finally back at the abbot, before crying, "Caw!"

Laughing loudly, Benedict gave the raven's head another stroke. "I thought so, little friend. I thought so." Looking at the timorous worshipers, he began to recite the words of the fourth Psalm:

"Answer me when I call, O God, defender of my cause; you set me free when I am hard-pressed; have mercy on me and hear my prayer. You mortals, how long will you dishonor my glory? How long will you worship dumb idols and run after false gods? Know that the Lord does wonders for the faithful; when I call upon the Lord, he will hear me. Tremble, then, and do not sin; speak to your heart in silence upon your bed. Offer the appointed sacrifices and put your trust in the Lord. Many are saying, 'Oh, that we might see better times!' Lift up the light of your countenance upon us, O Lord. You have put gladness in my heart, more than when grain and wine and oil increase. I lie down in peace; at once I fall asleep, for only you, Lord, make me dwell in safety."

Benedict looked out over the dozens of souls. Although some still exhibited fear, most showed resolve upon their faces, and all nodded as if embraced by the hands of courage. Benedict walked into the middle of the gathering, the raven still clinging to his left arm, and raised his right hand before speaking.

"Yes, we lack food. Yes, we are under threat. But the adversity we face is the opportunity the Lord shall work through marvelously. The victory will be ours if we wait upon the Lord Jesus with courage."

It was at dawn when Rodolfino opened the door to Benedict's room. "Father!" he hissed.

Benedict sat upon his bed.

"I am sorry to interrupt what you might be doing, but you need to come to the front gate."

"The Slavs have not approached the monastery?" Benedict asserted.

"Why do you ask that?" inquired Rodolfino.

Benedict stood up from his bed as the raven flew from the window sill and alighted on his left hand. The abbot walked across his small room and kindly touched Rodolfino on the shoulder. "Let us go to the gate, as you requested."

Heading through the door, Benedict paused and turned back as the raven let out a loud caw. "Christ's opportunity from our adversity. Come along with Peter and myself."

Rodolfino looked around to see where this 'Peter' was. Mystefied he followed Benedict and the raven out of the room.

"Father!" Rodolfino called as he and Benedict approached the gate. "It is truly a miracle! Whatever our fears are, they will vanish as the sun rises!"

"Calm yourself, Brother Rodolfino," Benedict answered, waving his right hand as Peter the raven let out another lengthy squawk. "I take it the Slavs are nowhere near?"

"That's just the thing, Father! We heard shouts in the valley as if their force was advancing up the mount, and then a mist arose from the forest obscuring the road. Some of us watched from the ramparts and heard new shouts, different calls...what sounded like yelps of fear. We heard swords unsheathed and shields battered. Cries of pain reached to the skies!"

"They must have grown confused and attacked each other in the fog," the judge gasped.

"That we assumed," said another of the monks, who jumped from a ladder adjoining the rampart to the ground, "for as the sun peeked over the horizon, we saw dead bodies at the base of the road! Father, Almighty God has indeed saved us!"

At that, the men gave a great cheer, and Peter the raven squawked once more!

"And that is not all," added Rodolfino, walking toward the gate and opening it wide. "Father, come see!"

Benedict shuffled forward. There, on the ground before him, lay twenty large cloth sacks, some loaded down with wheat, and some with baked bread. An awed hush fell over the other monks as Benedict smiled and then raised himself up to stand, the raven never leaving his arm.

"Bread and grain," he exulted, "enough to sustain us for weeks. The Lord knows our needs; the Lord provides for our every need. Today, brothers, we are saved from death and saved from hunger, for the Lord raises up His people. Let us remember this, that we are not ruled by our present worries, but by the promises of Christ in the past that are certain well into our future!"

The men shouted with glee and immediately rushed to bring the sacks of grain and bread into Monte Cassino. Leaving them to the task, Benedict climbed the ladder to the rampart, the raven still clinging to his arm, and he looked out over the expansive valley before turning to smile at the raven.

"A wondrous miracle, Peter," Benedict said. "Wouldn't you agree?"

Peter the raven let out another raucous "Caw!" Benedict could not help but laugh joyously in reply.

"Yes, Peter," he said. "With Christ before us, we go forward. Always forward." He breathed deeply as he smiled out over the countryside. "Everywhere forward."

BENEDICT was born in Nursia, Italy around 480, a twin with his devout sister Scholastica. His deep trust in Christ, combined with his energetic desire to nurture the faith of others, led him to found monasteries in and around the town of Subbiaco. His great literary achievement came in his Rule of St. Benedict, which laid out directives for monastery life that formed the activity of monks around physical labor, prayer, and obedience. This discipline set the standard for monasticism in western Europe through the Middle Ages, and it formed the heartbeat of his great monastery, Monte Cassino, which he founded around 529. Throughout the constant societal unrest and hardship of those years, Benedict remained faithful to Christ all the way to his death in 547.

FACT FILES

Medieval Monasticism

The years of the ancient church were marked by a considerable amount of energy. While Christians were establishing parameters for spiritual leadership, understanding how the New Testament took shape, or engaging in theological controversies that led to councils like Nicea and Chalcedon, there was barely a moment's time for the Church to catch its breath. Add in a considerable amount of early persecution, and we find that Christians faced the world with a great deal of vigor.

While no one dared declare that a Christian should be lazy or complacent, over time some leaders questioned what exactly God had called people to do. Throughout the late ancient church and into the Middle Ages, there arose an understanding that people might best serve God by joining communities dedicated to prayer and spiritual discipline. While these communities each had their own flavor and would develop into varied streams, they had a common vision to form a cluster of dedicated believers who withdrew from what they had known to a new life together. These communities became known as monasteries and the movement was monasticism.

Although we had just experienced some of Benedict's story at the monastery of Monte Cassino, the monastic movement predates him by a number of years. St. Antony of Egypt (251-356) was the first notable monk to gather followers into communities, centered mostly in the Egyptian desert and caves. Pachomius later built a physical monastery in Tabennisi, Egypt around the year 320, as a home for dedicated monks. Monasteries later experienced a surge of interest by virtue of the endorsement of Basil of Caesarea (330-379), who dictated that monasteries should be families of community, prayer, and work. Later monastic leaders such as John Cassian and Cassiodorus expanded the construction of monasteries into western Europe and emphasized the copying of ancient manuscripts for the preservation of classical and Biblical knowledge.

But it was Benedict who took the threads of monasticism and wove them together into a beautiful tapestry. In his Rule, Benedict effectively organized the life of his monasteries (and the entire order of what came to be known as the Benedictines). Believing that work disciplined the followers of Christ to serve Him better, Benedict ordered that part of the life of the monastery should be dedicated to physical labor. This would include gardening and growing the food eaten by the monks, enabling a level of self-sufficiency. Other monks might engage in craftsmanship and wood working or copying manuscripts. Some would keep the monastery buildings clean and well-swept. For every monk, there was an essential job to do. Worship was another portion of daily life, with many times set apart for prayer. Matins would occur at midnight, followed by Lauds three hours later, then—in regular increments—Prime, Tierce, Sext, Nones, Vespers, and Compline. A monk would pursue rest and sleep, when necessary, but prayer and worship were absolutely critical to the community's existence. And Benedict also demanded loving obedience to the abbot, the director of the monastery, as one would obey Christ Himself.

As the Church increased in stature and authority throughout the Middle Ages, the monastic movement experienced similar increases. To this end, there were positives and negatives as we evaluate medieval monasticism. Happily, there was a great deal of missionary fervor to take the Gospel of Jesus Christ to the surrounding areas. Monks were also able to put service into action. The manual labor of the Benedictines is a prime example, but there is also the matter of showing hospitality. In a world where one could not be certain of finding a decent inn to stay the night and where one might not want to risk sleeping on the open ground, monasteries would often allow travelers to stay in guest quarters for the night and receive food. Much of this grew out of Benedict's desire to receive every person as if receiving Jesus in one's presence. Monasteries served as schools and even hospitals for surrounding areas, and their collection of books became the libraries of the Middle Ages.

On the other hand, some negative realities grew up in monasticism. The reality of many sinners within a community meant that, sadly, one could find corruption, power-hungry leaders and followers, and some illicit behavior. Sometimes sons of nobles would opt to enter the monastic life and be upset that the activity there was more demanding and not as cushioned as they were used to. And after a time, a greater number of orders sprouted, each with its own emphasis, where it could seem there was much competition, depending on if one was aligned with the Benedictines, Franciscans, Dominicans, Augustinians, and so forth.

One of the key questions that we can pose regarding monasticism is, "Is withdrawal from the world to the monastery effective?" In one way, it is problematic. Why withdraw from the world when Jesus entered the world Himself to save us? Just because one withdraws from temptations and problems doesn't make one's heart pure when isolated. In other words, "wherever you go, there you are", and Jeremiah's reminder that "the heart is exceedingly wicked above all things"[1] rang true even to the most dedicated monks. Also, monasticism could raise the idea that serving Christ in the monastery was a higher calling than being a merchant or farmer or fisherman. The

1. Jeremiah 17:9

problem is the Bible nowhere claims this radical distinction between "sacred" and "secular" work. All proper work is godly if God has ordained it and we offer it to Him with glad hearts.

Despite the problems, these were challenges that would be faced by any movement seeking a new way of pleasing God. And while monasticism struggled to confront these challenges, there were plenty of leaders who met these challenges head-on. When things needed reforming and cleansing, those reactions usually came from within the monasteries themselves. And in a time when western civilization was under threat by economic collapse, war, and lack of education, monks kept the light of civilization alive through their dedicated work to preserve the best of Scriptural and classical teaching passed down through the ages. Our link to the past that gives us understanding for our present and future is found largely in the work of faithful monks, many of whom labored in obscurity while pursuing the glory of God.

COLUMBA

580, the Scottish island of Iona

"The sail! The sail" came the desperate shout of Caltram the sailor moments before the spray and foam covered him in the stern of the boat. The gale thumped against the wavering sail, causing it to shudder so badly that Talorc could have believed the earth had been shaken to its core. Slipping over the slick boards of the boat, Talorc snared the rope and pulled it so hard that his fists slammed into his rib cage. Fluttering against the howling blast, the sail braced and held firm even as the pain erupted in his side.

"I have it," Talorc cried as he inched closer to the mast, steadying his feet against its base. "Will we be able to get around those rocks?" he thought anxiously. Closing his eyes, he waited for the expected crunch and the splitting of boards, but none came. Looking once more, he was surprised to see Caltram throw his shoulder against the rudder to steer it away from the harrowing crag, back into the open sea before gently guiding it back.

Backing away three steps from the mast, Talorc turned to the sailor. "How on earth did you manage that?" he called into the wind.

"Long experience," Caltram replied before pointing straight ahead. "There's the spot! The high rocks around the bay will shield us from the wind, but I can't steer her all the way to shore."

"What to do, then?" Talorc shouted as he righted himself and looked for his satchel.

"I know the exact spot, young man. You see ahead where the beach ends on either side? Imagine a line joining the two places, and it'll be a boat's length past that line. I'll turn port side and you jump into the waves. The surf should carry you in, and see...looks like you have someone expecting you."

Talorc looked toward the beach and saw a lean man in a brown cloak, huddled over a pile of what looked like rocks and wood and fussing over something in that heap.

"Soon, then?" he called to Caltram, who nodded and steered the boat forward. Another man then came forward to take the rudder.

"My shipmate will take the back end now," he yelled above the wind. "Give me the sail-rope and prepare to jump. Then we can get this slab of wood turned and head back to Mull."

Talorc clutched his pack to his chest and placed a foot up near the bowsprit. He looked back at Caltram, who nodded and called, "Now! Jump! And God bless!"

The freezing waves cut against Talorc's skin like a hundred knives of ice. He gulped as a wall of water pushed him under, and for a moment he thought he would keep plunging downward, losing breath for good. Then he felt a hand grasp him around the scruff of his neck before he lost consciousness.

The sky was considerably lighter when Talorc opened one eye, his cheek scratching against coarse sand and his nose sniffing a glorious smell of fish and bread. Pushing his hands into the beach and raising himself off the ground, he turned his head and felt his neck crack with relief. Sputtering furiously, he dislodged a piece of seaweed from his mouth and coughed again more productively.

"Ah," came a voice from the fire, "you survived! I was quite worried you wouldn't live to see breakfast, but now we have a fellow partaker for the meal!"

Talorc struggled to sit up before taking in the scene around him. Several men in similar cloaks scurried around the fire, placing large stones near it to act as seats. One came up to Talorc and threw a dry blanket around him.

"Come and join us and dry yourself over breakfast," he said in a welcoming voice. "Welcome to Iona, by the way."

"Thank you," Talorc replied, stumbling to the fire and setting himself upon a broad, flat stone. He let loose a shiver just as the lean man in the brown cloak approached with a kindly smile and a bowl of pan-smoked fish and bread.

"Good morning!" he exclaimed, a wisp of his wavy, dark hair flapping against his forehead in the stiff breeze "God be praised for your survival of the sea. I trust you had no difficulty finding our abode."

"If this is Iona," Talorc exclaimed, "you must be Columba. I am Talorc."

"This is Iona and I am Columba, and this is your breakfast," Columba declared, handing the bowl to Talorc. "But first, we give thanks." And with those words, the four other men immediately stopped their activity and bowed their heads with Columba who tented his fingers together.

"We bless you, Almighty God," he called aloud, "Whose power extends over sea and land, and whose angels watch over us all. We pray for peace as we do our daily work, gathering seaweed, catching fish, baking bread, praying, chanting, reading, and quieting our hearts, always thanking you. We bless you for the gift of this breakfast, and for the gift of a new soul to share in it and in your work here. Delightful it is to live on this peaceful isle, in simple lives, serving you, the King of Kings, in whose name we pray. Amen."

"Amen," repeated the men, including Talorc, who waited until Columba sat next to him before asking, "How did you know?"

"How did I know what?" Columba replied, his eyes twinkling.

"That I came here to live and seek to do God's work?"

Columba laughed. "My son, why does anyone turn into this bay and jump from a boat to come to land unless they were drawn here by our Heavenly Father?" He shook his head and laughed. "But I get ahead of myself. You need to gather your strength after that savage swim. Let us take our breakfast, and then on our way back to the abbey, I can tell you my story."

"You do not need to hear mine?" asked Talorc.

"That I will come to discover as you work among us, my son," Columba replied, "but it is only fair that if you have come here to do the Lord's work, that you know of why I came here to establish it."

The party shuffled along the ground up from the bay. Iona was a rugged isle, a green jewel carved out of the ocean, and though it was small, the path back to the abbey called for steady and strong feet. The others walked a bit ahead of Columba and Talorc as the former began to tell his tale.

"You have heard of this place, dear Talorc," he began, "but perhaps not how it came to be. We live in great austerity here, which some might find strange for a former member of the Irish royal clan."

"You were of the great nobles of Eire?" Talorc replied, amazed.

Columba nodded. "My father Phelim McFergus was part of the O'Neill royal family, and my mother Ethne descended from the Cheinnselaig kings of Leinster. As such, I was fostered by a priest for my education and training. Cruithnechan was his name, and he taught, reared, and baptized me. It was he who actually forced me to take daily walks and runs in the hills for some fresh air

INVERNESS

SCOTLAND

GLASGOW

EDINBURGH

IONA

because I was so determined to stay inside the church and read the Psalms!"

"You have been living for this your entire life then, Columba," Talorc remarked.

"In truth I have, though I did not know that path would take me here," he replied ruefully. "Cruithnechan believed I needed deeper training in the Scriptures if I would train as a priest, so he sent me to Moville on the Irish coast, to study under Finnian. It was he who taught me to read and study through the books of Scripture. I could see God's Word come to life. The journey from our sin to our redemption in Christ was written for us! That way I could read in the Gospels what the sacrifices in Leviticus and the kings of David's line prepared us to encounter, the risen Christ! I was on a never-ending quest for deeper waters from which to drink. I ended up at Clonard and, instead of being taught, I began teaching others. We went out and established schools and monasteries throughout Ireland, from Derry to Durrow to Kells and all over. I transcribed manuscripts, wrote commentaries on Scripture, and devoted every waking moment to ensuring fellow priests could shed the light of Christ all over Ireland." He paused and stood still. "My vigor continued, my activity never slowed down, and I was hailed as the godliest and most scholarly Christian in generations." And here he looked quite crestfallen.

Talorc stopped with him, noting a tear working its way down Columba's cheek. "For you to speak of the heights of your vocation with such grief," Talorc uttered, "tells me there is a terrible moment that changed everything."

Columba looked up at the gray sky and then tenderly at Talorc. "Yes," he replied, shuffling onward as they reached the top and entered the wide plain, "something that changed my heart forever. I was so zealous for knowledge and Scriptural wisdom that I sought the best texts to copy.

In my haste, I copied a manuscript of Jerome's that was brought from Rome. Finnian was furious."

"Your master at Moville?"

"Yes, Finnian erupted in rage over my zeal. I had copied it without his permission, and he ordered me to return the text to him. Prideful for my place in the eyes of others, I refused, and so Finnian went to the high king of Tara, Diarmat mac Cerbaill, who happened to be my kinsman. I was certain family would reward family, but the high king ruled against me."

"And did you return the manuscript?"

Columba swallowed. "I am ashamed that I did not. Eventually Finnian and I resolved our differences, but Diarmat and I did not. I viewed his sentence as overly harsh and he would not relinquish it. The king said, 'To every cow belongs her calf, and to each book belongs its copy.' He called me and my family traitors to our land. I refused to back down to this slight, and Tara and O'Neill went to war."

"Over the copy?"

"Yes, and I bear the blame for churning my kin into a frenzy and going into battle. We met on the field at Cul Dreimhne, near Sligo, and the day rained down the blood of many. Our forces won the battle, but my cousin Aed was in my grasp as I was pulling him to safety when a Tara soldier struck his head with a club. I watched him die as others swarmed the killer and finished him off. Oh, Talorc, I wept and wept and wept! Three thousand men fell that day, and for what? Because I stubbornly would not part with a copy I had made? Because I wanted my name to be elevated above all others for renown and honor?"

Columba's steps slowed as the abbey now rose ahead of them. "That night, mothers and wives wept for their fallen as I wandered away from the camp and poured out my heart to Christ above. I knew the price for this devastation must be paid, and I must pay that price. I was to become an exile for Christ and leave my native Ireland, to a place where I could lead others to save lives as I was responsible for the loss of others. I was to build a place to train men so we could venture out and claim surrounding lands for the Gospel of our Lord. To win to Christ as many—no, more!—lives than were lost at Cul Dreimhne!

"And so we set off from Derry, myself with twelve others, as the disciples of Christ. We sailed in our currach[1] until we reached this rocky jewel in the midst of a raging sea, this Iona. It was nineteen years ago today that we arrived and set about building."

"It is quite a monastery, Columba," admitted Talorc.

"No, not a monastery to escape from the world," Columba cautioned, wagging his finger slowly, "but a community by which we shall be unleashed for the glory of Christ in the wild and unpredictable power of the Holy Spirit. It is here that we live and work and train. Work, prayer, study. This will be your life as you prepare to go out, good Talorc, wherever that may be. You might find yourself amongst the Scots, the Picts, other pagans or to the distant continent itself. But if you would live among us, do so in the wood and thatch huts you see, my son. Stay in the guest house for now, but know we walk in discipline sprinkled generously with Christian love and brotherhood. There will be hard tasks of gardening and washing, of crafting things with your hands, before you find regular labor in the scriptorium or before you ever lead prayers. This life is not comfortable, and I hold myself to that above all. I sleep on a bare rock and a stone for a pillow. The life is austere but simple. A hut for each participant. A refectory for eating our meals. A forge for metalworking and making shoes for our farm horses. A kiln. A mill for our grain and threshing. The barns for the animals. The scriptorium where we keep our many manuscripts. And of course, here we have the church."

1. A currach is a type of small Irish boat with a wooden wicker frame, over which animal skins or hides were stretched

They walked in, joining the men who had already arrived. Talorc looked above and around him, taking in the sight of the simple yet beautiful structure. The colored portraits on the walls. The high stone cross at the front of the nave. What a place to live, thought Talorc. What a place to draw near to the Christ who has saved me.

"Well, Talorc," Columba said, breaking the silence and sweeping his hand toward the other men. "What do you think?"

Talorc nodded and bowed to them. "It's perfect. And if God wills and you are willing, I will stay."

"My son, this community was birthed out of my own grievous sin," Columba sighed. "What we find is that no one is beyond the grasp of the Lord Jesus. Not us. And most certainly not those to whom we will be sent."

Columba raised his hands and turned to the cross, with Talorc and the others bowing the heads with him as he prayed aloud:

"Be a bright flame before us, O God, a guiding star above us. Be a smooth path below us, a kindly shepherd behind us, today, tonight, and forever. Alone with You, our God, we journey on our way. What do we fear when You are near, O Lord of night and day? More secure are we within Your hand than if a multitude around us did stand. Amen."[2]

COLUMBA's missionary work transformed the British Isles into a beacon for the Gospel of Christ. His vision to claim for God's Kingdom more souls than were lost in the fateful Battle of Cul Dreimhne was realized many times over through his work at Iona. The abbey there became the greatest missionary training center in history, equipping men to learn and proclaim Scripture with a zeal to travel to pagan areas and call people to the Lord Jesus Christ.

2.http://www.spiritofsaintandrews.org.uk/prayer-for-those-coming-to-or-exploring-faith/the-prayer-of-st-columba/

Columba himself evangelized King Brude and his Pictish kingdom in Scotland, bringing grace and peace to the lives of Scottish citizens. His simple and direct preaching came out of a life of both learning Scripture and copying manuscripts of the Bible so others could have God's Word. His kind-hearted and practical faith inspired Iona to remain an energetic center of missionary endeavor even beyond his death in 597.

IONA

GREGORY THE GREAT

April 593, Rome

The humble man, clad in a dusty red robe and looking worriedly about, stepped through the narrow streets of the city. Lips moving briskly in silent prayer, the issues of his heart poured out as he beheld what lay before him. Filth on the ground, the cries of starving babies wafting from open windows, mangy dogs limping around them, and the wretched smell of standing water that had pooled for days in the alleyways. Although Easter had come and gone without much joyous fanfare, the people of Rome could hardly believe better days were coming.

The robed priest stumbled on, slipping on loose stones but finally making it to the smooth-laned street paralleling the west back of the Tiber River, within sight of St. Peter's Basilica. He looked up as he approached the magnificent edifice. Nearly four thousand worshipers could fit in here if they desired, he thought, and yet therein lies the trouble. Finding the desire is so fleeting. There were many heartaches pockmarking his days, difficulties he imagined would be common to one in this position. Little wonder, Gregory thought, that he had begged in writing that the bishops take back their decision to name him pope. And they had refused, and he reluctantly agreed to face the days ahead by God's strength.

As he took the steps in front of the basilica one by one as the deacon shuffled out of the church's interior and approached him. "Holy Father, we have heard from a contingent of messengers from the Lombard camp outside the walls. They desire that we hand over the city to them. At that point, they will consider relieving the suffering of our people, but only for the price of possession of Rome."

Gregory nodded briefly, then moved past him into St. Peter's. "Very well, my son. Let us pray to the Lord in the meantime."

"Did you not hear what I said?" exclaimed the stunned priest. "We are facing disaster!"

"All the more reason to pray at a time like this," Gregory insisted as he continued on into the heart of the church.

"Hear us, Lord, and bring Thy mercy, for against Thee we have sinned.

Hear us, Lord, and bring Thy mercy, for against Thee we have sinned.

To Thee, O Most High, Redeeming King,
With tears of woe we lift our eyes:
Hear, O Lord, your sinful servants' prayers.

Hear us, Lord, and bring Thy mercy, for against Thee we have sinned.

Hear us, Lord, and bring Thy mercy, for against Thee we have sinned."

The echo of their chants faded as they both bowed before the altar. The priest closed and then opened his eyes before breaking the silence.

"You were right, Holy Father, to insist on prayer first. I ask forgiveness for my lack of faith. When uncertainty erupts around us, our first thought should be toward our Savior's throne, not our plans for rescue."

"Your impulse was entirely natural," Gregory replied. "You have a keen mind and strategic approach. I think eventually it will serve you well in many ways."

"Away from Rome?"

Gregory shrugged as they drew near to his papal apartments. "Our Lord promised His disciples would take the Gospel to the ends of the earth. Perhaps you'd consider Britain?" He saw the confused look on the priest's face. "Ah, well. Let's not speak of that here." He entered the room and gathered some papers from his desk. "Come with me."

"Those papers, Holy Father," the priest mentioned as they went back through the church and aimed for the middle of the five entry doors. "They grow thicker every day. Is this your commentary on Ezekiel or something else?"

Gregory slowed his pace, walking deliberately through the great church. "I truly believe, my son," Gregory replied after several moments of thought, "that we are in extraordinarily unique times. Christ is calling us forth, and if we are walking toward Him every action we take in faith. We will either sink or swim depending on our response."

"Faith and response?"

"That is how I see faith," the pope replied. "God kindly captures us in His grace. We take Him at His Word, and then we must act upon it." He showed the sheaves of papers to his friend. "It begins with we who have spiritual authority, and for that I wrote this Rule eighteen months ago."

"Like Benedict's Rule?"

"Like it, yet unlike it. Yes, it is a pattern for action and life together, but not for those under authority. Rather, I think we who serve as bishops of Christ's Church need to wake up to a new identity. We tend to act like the spiritual nobility, as if we are owed honor and standing. I argue in these pages that we who are bishops are actually shepherds. The pastors and people who populate our churches are our sheep. Yes, they require the occasional tap with a shepherd's crook, but we are to oversee and love them, feeding them with the Word of Christ, nourishing them with the chants of worship, tending to them when they are tired and harassed. It is a message I intend to send to all bishops throughout our empire, as the primary head of Christ's Church. And it is a belief I intend to put into action right now."

Gregory suddenly began walking toward the door as the priest followed him. "Holy Father, where are we going then?"

"To the monastery just beyond our little wall here," the pope pointed as they pushed through the door. "I need to have a talk with several of the monks, Bishop Demetrius of Naples, and Patriarch Severus of Aquileia. We need to have it now."

"With the bishop and the patriarch? How will they get past the enemy lines even if we had sent them word weeks ago?"

Gregory gave a smile and a wink as he opened the door to the monastery. "They have been here for months in shelter. Demetrius came seeking wisdom, Severus seeking escape from the Lombards before they took Venice. See," he pointed in the direction of two men stooped near a fire that cooked some sort of meat stew, "there they are."

"Holy Father," Demetrius called from the darkness of the refectory as Severus rose to his feet and other monks crowded around.

"Good evening, fellow servants of Christ," Gregory responded. "We are weary of the siege and of the travails of our present days, but we will not be weary in well-doing. Today, we take seriously what I intend to be an all-encompassing desire for service. For years we have been used to more comfort than pain; today, the people within our walls of Rome are suffering immeasurably, and we will all join them in their pain and seek to relieve their suffering at the same time."

"Holy Father," Demetrius groaned, "while I appreciate your desire to quell what ails this city, do you need us to assist in what you ask? It is a rather tiring affair, after all."

"My dear Demetrius," Gregory said calmly, although his gentle tone hid his frustration, "you are not sauntering through fine vineyards in the Neapolitan valley, nor are you selecting which rich vestments to wear for Mass. You are a servant of the Most High God and King of Heaven. You represent Christ to the people who are under your care for the good of their souls. Our Lord Jesus Himself did not consider equality with His Father as a laurel to wear with pride, but He came amongst us on earth to live among us, obeying perfectly where we could not and dying the death we deserved. If dwelling among us was not too great for Christ, why would any of us complain about such a—as you put it—tiring affair?"

Demetrius looked away into the fire, thoroughly and properly chastised, and said nothing, nodding that he understood perfectly.

"If this is the case," Severus asked, "what are our duties?"

"One of the assisting priests will show you," Gregory replied, "but we have need for each man among us, from myself to the scribes and kitchen hands, to take the wagons of bread and vegetables to every district of Rome. I am grateful to God that we had arranged for the food to be delivered from the surrounding farmlands before the Lombards arrived. There are thirty of us and fifteen horse-drawn wagons outside the stables, so that will be a ratio of two men to every cart."

Demetrius smiled, "You paid attention to mathematics in your schooling more than I."

Gregory grinned, happy the previous tension between them had passed. "Let us go forth. We are servants of God and shepherds to His people. May we show ourselves worthy of the task."

"Is there a reason why you and I are distributing near the gates, Holy Father?" asked another of the leaders of the monastery's scriptorium.

"This area does contain some rather destitute and desperate families," Gregory acknowledged as several loaves of bread and an armload of carrots were handed to a woman clutching a baby. Nodding, Gregory waved a blessing and said, "May God watch over you, dear one!"

"Thank you, Father!" the woman whispered hoarsely.

Turning to one of the monks, Gregory asked, "You are sure the monastery can afford these reserves?"

"Yes, Father, as God wills," was the reply. "If need be, we'll make thinner stew with fewer potatoes and less chicken."

Gregory looked up at the ramparts of the walls. "Truth be told, I also had a selfish reason for coming this way," he admitted. Gesturing toward a large gate, he waved at a centurion who had been speaking to one of his subordinates. "I'd like to see if we have any chance to speak to the Lombards directly."

The others were stunned to hear this plan.

Just then a centurion hailed him, "Holy Father! How glad I am of your arrival. I have made contact with the king and queen of the Lombards to meet you outside."

"With Agilulf and Theodelinda?" the pope replied.

One of the church leaders hissed stridently. "Holy Father, have you lost your senses?"

"By the juniper tree about an arrow's strike away from the wall," the centurion said. "I'll escort you there under flag of truce."

"With a good will," Gregory responded. Turning to his astonished companions he declared, "Please distribute the remainder of the food. I will see you back at the monastery after nightfall."

The two figures by the juniper tree could not be more different in personality. Agilulf the king scowled impatiently, while Theodelinda his bride glowed with happiness at Gregory's approach with the centurion at his side. Holding out her hands and taking Gregory's own while flashing a marvelous smile, Theodelinda waited while Gregory offered a slight bow.

"Holy Father, we thank you for your willingness to come," Agilulf spoke gruffly as he wiped his hands and drew near to the pope. "Your passion to save and maintain your people in these dire circumstances is most impressive." The king looked to Rome's walls, as if wary that an arrow could fly from the battlements. "I will also say that despite the vigor, you must be the first to know the Romans have exhausted their efforts. I have marched this army over mountain and valley for God and glory. Do not stand between me and my conquest. Give this place and your churches over to us. I beg you. Aren't you weary of the endless squalor within your walls? Your political leaders are powerless and hate the very idea of open battle. To bear the weight of temporal power along with spiritual authority is too much for you to bear. I pray you would listen to reason and surrender the city."

Gregory listened earnestly, his hands behind his back. When Agilulf ended his speech, the pope straightened and looked him in the eye.

"My dear King Agilulf, if you were truly desiring all you asked, your queen would not be here."

Agilulf looked aghast, but sputtered, "Whatever do you mean?"

"Just this, good king: I have known your wife before she married you. I was not keen on your union due to your rejection of Christ as God, but believed Theodelinda might win you by her charm and humility. If you were truly ready to claim the city of Rome, you would have attacked by now. Your queen is the tether that holds you back from the destruction of these walls. The question is why."

"Holy Father, please," the queen urged. "Help him to see reason."

Gregory stepped toward Agilulf and placed his hands on his shoulders. “Dear king, you do not see Jesus as the divine One, whereas I worship Him as Savior, Lord, and God. But imagine how Jesus Himself is saddened by this unnecessary slaughter! King Agilulf,” Gregory wept, his voice faltering as the king tried to look away, “is this the path of Jesus? Would God our Father do as you wish to do? When the Son of God came into this world, His kingdom did not come with battle-cry or fiery arrows or the sound of clashing swords. He is called the Prince of Peace for good reason. Whether you fall at His feet now, or in future years, or on your deathbed, do you believe that what you have requested gives Him joy or pain?”

And there it was. Gregory saw a tear moisten in the corner of Agilulf's eye. Theodelinda clutched at her husband's arm. “My love,” she whispered, “please consider.”

Agilulf nodded and clasped Gregory's hand. “I cannot turn away with nothing, you know. A king cannot return empty-handed.”

“I agree,” Gregory assented, “and so this is what is offered: Claim the lands and pasture in this region for your people. Take one-fourth of the crops for a tax. Your court may have access to the city as needed. But the Catholic Church shall worship Christ as we always have. On that point, there is no compromise.”

Theodelinda looked at the pope, then the king. “Do we have an accord?”

Agilulf's face broke into a toothy grin, as if relieved the strain was over. “We have an accord.” He shook Gregory's hand, adding, “Blessed are you, Holy Father. I must say I am impressed by your courage. Your city and your church are in your good hands.”

Shaking his head, Gregory waved off the compliment as he bowed in homage to Agilulf. “Not my city, and not my church. They both belong to Almighty God.”

Gregory the Great

Pope **GREGORY THE GREAT** reigned during a unique time and brought a unique set of gifts and talents to the papacy in Rome. A great preacher, Gregory was also a dedicated reformer of worship, writing a number of chants and songs. He also brought about strong changes in the roles of bishops; his *Pastoral Rule* directed bishops to work at the craft of preaching and to be shepherds of their people rather than nobles who lived off the Church. Turning his strong personality toward the troubles in western Europe, Gregory also stepped in where kings proved ineffective, negotiating peace with invading armies like the Lombards to secure peace for the people of Rome.

FACT FILES

The Dual Rise of the Papacy and Islam

In the early Middle Ages so far, we have traced the rise of monks and missions, and we will later see these lead to a revival of classical learning in schools and monasteries. Aside from the individuals and personalities we have encountered so far, two movements were growing in Europe, the Middle East, and north Africa, and these two movements couldn't be more different. Centered in Europe, we see the Popes of the Roman Catholic Church beginning to gain more and more power. In the Middle East and north Africa, the new religion of Islam aggressively spreads through force and conquest.

The office of pope, often called the papacy, began a slow and steady increase in influence. Leo I (400-461) was the first bishop of Rome to assert that the Pope there inhabited a place of primacy, one who stood above the other bishops in the Christian world, due to the apostolic succession from receiving the power of spiritual rule that went back to the apostle Peter. In time, future popes began to grow this influence in greater measure. Some did so through their pastoral gifts. Gregory I, whom we previously mentioned, gave wise direction on worship, preaching, and how bishops and priests should conduct themselves. He also helped defend Rome against enemy invaders and wrote a biography of Benedict. His energy and actions alone made for a great pope. But others would also assert the primacy of the papacy by declaring it in different ways. Even before Gregory's reign, a pope named Gelasius I (died 496) used biblical teaching about Jesus to defend the power of the Pope. As Jesus had both a divine nature and a human nature, Gelasius said, "So too do we have sacred government (the Church) and secular government (kings and emperors) to exercise authority over people." Gelasius went a step further by saying that when there is a conflict between these two governments, it is the Church that has the primacy and overrules secular government. And since the Roman pope, he said—following Leo's teaching—is the highest leader in the Church, he is the greatest leader in the Christian world, over kings and emperors.

Obviously, not every king willingly went along with this. And not every pope was as strong as Gelasius or Gregory. Some popes showed dominating power and authority. Gregory VII (pope from 1073 to 1085) forced Holy Roman Emperor Henry IV to accept that the church, not emperors, had the power to name bishops. He used the force of his personality to greatly enforce clerical celibacy (the rule that priests should not marry) in the Catholic Church, and he also ended the practice of simony, where men would secure high positions in the Church by paying large sums of money. Innocent III (pope from 1198 to 1216) was another of the powerful popes of the Middle Ages. He expanded the military might of the Church through crusades against Muslims in the Middle East and against radical heretics in France. He recognized the Franciscan order of monks under Francis of Assisi, and Innocent was also willing to force his will upon kings like John of England, declaring that sacraments, baptisms, and funerals could not be performed in England until John repented of his rebellion.

While the authority of the popes strengthened at many points in the West, another force was rising in the Middle East. In the seventh century, the tribes of the Arabian peninsula followed a variety of pagan gods. Disgusted by the multitude of gods and the immorality he perceived among his people; a merchant named Muhammed would periodically retreat to a cave near his home city of Mecca. According to Muhammad, one night during the year 610, the angel Gabriel (who had announced to the Virgin Mary that she would become the mother of Jesus) appeared to him and began dictating to Muhammad what would become the Qur'an. This volume of collected words would become the holy book for Muhammad's newly founded religion, Islam. Coming from the Arabic word for "submission" or "surrender", Islam's followers would become known as Muslims, "those who submit". Muhammad's decree was that people should submit to the will of the one god, Allah, of whom Muhammad was his chief prophet.

Islam laid significant emphasis on the doing of good works that demonstrated faithfulness to Allah. Chapters within the Qur'an also bore some similarities with Jewish and Christian religion—namely, that there is only one God and (in connection with Christianity) the importance of Jesus. However, in Islam, Jesus is not the Savior of those who trust in Him by faith for their salvation from sin. In Islam, people bear the entire responsibility of keeping their works good so that it pleases Allah. Christians embrace the loving hope that Jesus paid the penalty for their sin on the cross, and we live holy lives because Christ earned God's favor for us, not to earn God's favor ourselves. In Islam, Jesus is a major prophet, second only behind Muhammad, but He is not God's eternal Son and is not divine. Christians know that Jesus is the Son, the second Person of the Trinity who exists eternally as God. In time, most Muslims came to believe Jesus never died on the cross. One popular Muslim view was that Judas, guilt-ridden over his betrayal of Jesus, died on the cross instead; Christians teach that Jesus' crucifixion is absolutely essential; there is no salvation without it. Although Muslims say Allah is merciful, the Qur'an paints a portrait that emphasizes the stern, resolute, unyielding aspects of God's character, who simply sends guidance through prophets but does not come to the world in person. The Christian faith looks to the Bible, where God is revealed as loving Father and the Seeker of His wandering sheep, who will do anything to chase them down and embrace them.

Within months, Muhammad managed to convert Arabia partly through military conquest and establish the power of Islam throughout the land, with the center of the faith located in the city of Mecca. After his death in 632, the new leaders of Islam turned the religion into a conquest-driven faith. Within a few decades, Muslim armies swept over north Africa, Palestine (taking Jerusalem), Persia, Syria, and large swaths of the Byzantine Empire that Constantine had founded and strengthened so many years before. Although holding out for a time, eventually the capital of Constantinople fell to the Muslim Turks in 1453[1]. With an eye to taking Europe, Islamic warriors had crossed the Straits of Gibraltar and plunged into Spain, invading that land and establishing dominion there in 711 (Muslims who settled in medieval Spain were called Moors). Seeking additional land in the name of Allah, Moorish armies moved into southern France, hoping to constrict the power of European kingdoms and encircle the old Roman territory completely. It might have happened if not for a key clash in October 732 in the chilly countryside of France. With fury and passion, the Frankish king Charles Martel utterly defeated Moorish troops at the Battle of Tours. Withstanding a cavalry charge on the high ground, Martel sent his army into the sides of the Moorish columns, and his heavily-clothed men swarmed over the unprepared, lightly-clad Moors. Subsequent raids and victories drove the Moors out of France and back into Spain, preventing a full conquest of European soil.

From then on, the Catholics in the West and the Muslims in the East dwelt separately, building their power and authority while keeping an uneasy eye on one another. It would be less than four centuries after Tours that the powder keg would explode once again with the Crusades.

---

1. The Byzantine Empire is the Eastern half of the Roman Empire/

THEODULF

March 819, Angers, France

Placing his right hand against the wall of the turreted tower, the young monk stabilized his footing on the next step while clutching the small tray of food in his left grip. André fought to keep the apple from rolling off the tray while simultaneously preventing the cabbage soup from slopping out of the bowl. Righting himself, he was able to follow the mounted candles up the stairwell to the room where he'd been directed. The correct room, he thought. Red-painted latch and a whitewashed cross on the frame above. André cleared his throat and knocked clearly yet respectfully, intending to be heard but not obnoxious.

"Come in," a creaky, kind voice called from the inside. André pressed down the latch and entered the room. Two candles burned in the cozy interior. Pushing himself up from the chair at the desk, a tall, firmly muscled man, wearing a black cowl over his evening garments, placed a book onto his bed and took slow but sure steps in the direction of his visitor. Instinctively, André realized this was no ordinary man, no overnight guest.

"Good sir," André uttered as the cowled figure came toward him. "I've brought you dinner. It is not lavish, but the stew and an apple, with some bread, might suffice."

"My son, I thank you for your kindness," the older man rasped. "And how shall I address you by name?"

André suddenly recalled his forgetfulness. "Oh, I should have introduced myself! My name is André, a novice. I've recently entered this abbey. And I have also forgotten to bring your cup of cider along with your meal. Please forgive me and allow me to return to the refectory to fetch it."

"There is no need," the man insisted, reaching out and taking André's arm while directing him to place the food on the small table. "No need at all, André. Please do not trouble yourself. I have a small amount of water and that will be enough. What would be more enjoyable is if you remained here with me as I ate. I would be glad of company this evening."

"Well, I had no order to return immediately," André admitted, ""and I have no need to be on duty elsewhere... excuse me, I have neglected to discover your name."

"Because I was negligent in telling you, André," the man replied. "Forgive my manners. I am Theodulf."

André sat in a low chair, facing Theodulf. "I have not met you before today, Sir. Have you been here for some time?"

"Since last year. I was sent here from Orleans." Theodulf said quietly, although André could sense his heartfelt pain.

"Sent here? To Angers? From Orleans?" André replied. "And just last..." He stopped, hardly believing what he'd heard. "Not Bishop Theodulf of Orleans!"

"Well, my name is Theodulf, and I did live there..."

André nearly fell out of his chair from the surprise that he was face to face with the famed bishop of Orleans. "I ... I can scarcely believe it's true. You've been living here all this time, and I never knew?"

"For nearly a year, André," Theodulf said gently. "You do not mind if I ask the Lord to bless my meal?"

"Not at all," André replied excitedly, waiting for Theodulf to murmur his prayer of gratitude and then rejoin their conversation.

"You have found this monastery to be a gracious community?" asked Theodulf.

"Yes, in my short time here. From an early age I desired to serve Christ more than anything. Many events worked together to bring me to that point. I never thought I would end up in Angers, but I am glad God brought me here."

"I know something of what you speak," Theodulf responded. "I myself never dreamed I would be here, but events worked together—as you would say—to make that happen."

"If I may ask what are you, as the bishop of Orleans, doing living here?" André asked. "I thought you were serving the king himself."

"Ah, that," Theodulf mused as he broke bread and dipped a portion into his stew, placing the soppy bite in his mouth. "I was. That is past. I am not surprised that you did not know. I ordered the abbot not to tell my story to anyone. Angers has a good reputation for discretion and I wanted to preserve that. But you are right. I once labored on behalf of God and the king. Now, I serve God alone."

"What happened, your Grace?" André asked. "This is the last place I'd expect you to be."

Theodulf looked at the candle at his bedside, then back to André. "It is a long way from my former labors," he said. "Charles the Great, the one we all knew as Charlemagne... he convinced me to come from Spain for a great calling. I believed with all my heart this was God's clear direction."

"My mother said," remarked André, "that because of Charlemagne's orders, we were able to read Greek and Latin and the greatest of books. Without him, no such opportunity would exist."

"Your mother spoke the truth," Theodulf said before taking a gulp of water. "Charlemagne could command by the force of his very being and his weighty intentions. I remember when the pope crowned him on Christmas day almost nineteen years ago ... the first Holy Roman Emperor. Charlemagne, seven feet tall, knelt, nearly dwarfing the pope himself. But though forceful, the king always wanted the best for his people. And so, he turned to people like Alcuin, whom he brought from York, and to me. 'If the people are educated,' he would say, 'their souls will be truly liberated.'"

André nodded. "That is why my sister and I were taught to read, to write, to learn mathematics and astronomy. I still have my copy of Ptolemy's *Almagest* from the village church school in my hometown." Theodulf stared kindly at André and then went on. "Yes, I desired to fulfill the king's vision. I believed the best places to do that were schools that would be publicly open and which met within the town churches. The monasteries have done well in educating the elite, but we needed new avenues to reach as many of the people as possible, even those who could not pay. All through Orleans. Checy. Ormes. Combleux. Jargeau. Artenay ..."

"And Rebrechien," André added, "my school."

And here Theodulf looked wistful. "Ah, Rebrechien," he said, "The little school in the Eglise Notre-Dame. That was your school?"

"It was," André admitted, but slightly puzzled. He was certain that Theodulf was keeping back something. But what could it be? He asked another question, "But you kept your place at Orleans through Charlemagne's entire reign! What brought you here?"

"Abbot Remy knows," Theodulf began, "however, he has resolved to keep much of it to himself so I might dwell in peace. But I will tell you the story. Just please keep what I share private."

"I will."

Theodulf took another bite of stew and went on. "It happened two years ago in King Louis' court. King Louis is a capable emperor, but he is nothing like his father. I don't know if you are aware of his nephew, King Bernard, who was king of the Lombards. No? Well, King Bernard came to Aachen and joined us in King Louis' court when a striking incident occurred. We were worshiping on Maundy Thursday[1] two years ago when the roof of the church collapsed, and King Louis was nearly pinned beneath the rubble. He is, as I said, capable; however, he could be quite suspicious of the smallest of tragedies. King Louis began to think that there were people in his court plotting against him, to remove him as emperor. When he made a decree about those who might succeed him, he left King Bernard off that list. Needless to say, his cousin did not take that well and began mobilizing his Lombard army back home. King Louis captured King Bernard soon after, accused him of treason, and condemned him to death. In a moment of what King Louis termed as mercy, he ordered that his cousin should only have his eyes put out. I spoke out against such reprehensible behavior and King Louis turned on me violently, proceeding with the sentence of blinding. And matters went from horrible to tragic; King Bernard did not survive the savage action and died after only two days. Many voices spoke up in protest, including mine. I knew I was sealing my fate. King Louis had hardly treated me or the Church with the dignity and awe that Charlemagne his father had. I knew what I would lose, and yet I could not side with an unspeakable evil."

"I am surprised," André said in reply, "that in King Louis' state, he did not order you killed as well."

"I believe I survived and was given only exile for two reasons," Theodulf answered thoughtfully. "In the first place, there is still much respect for those of the old order who served under Charlemagne. It does not mean we aren't subject to unfair judgment, but there are limits on what King Louis might do out of fear for how the people might react. And secondly, and more importantly, I believe God

1. The Thursday prior to Easter Sunday, in which some churches remember Jesus' actions at the Last Supper with his disciples the night before his death.

still has me alive because He desired my continued labor on behalf of the Church."

"Even though you were stripped of your position as bishop?" André asked, not understanding Theodulf's calm and reserve.

"Oh, André," Theodulf smiled, waving his hands about, "one does not need to be a bishop to serve Christ well. To believe that higher position is the same as greater impact in God's world is to fall for deception. If you take this bowl back to the refectory and wash it, and if you take the core of this apple into the monastery's vast glade and plant it in the hopes a tree will arise, you have done as much if not more than a bishop who says a thousand Masses and preaches hundreds of sermons. There was going to come a day, whether I stepped down from my position or died, when I would no longer be bishop of Orleans. If King Louis would strip me of that, then it is for God to judge him, not me. Almighty God who is perfectly wise, just, and merciful will deal with King Louis far better than I could. I am content to have been exiled here, for it has given me time to meditate on the expanse of a life lived for Christ's name."

"It still seems rotten and unjust," André averred, "but what do you do in your work here? Meditation and prayer?"

"A good bit of that, yes. And I have a private seat when we gather in the chapel for prayers, out of the line of sight for most monks, so as not to draw attention. But lately I have been thinking about my past days, when I taught children around the area of Orleans, the Scriptures I explained. And I have realized that Almighty God might have given me greater understanding than ever before about my circumstances. Namely, that I see more than ever before how I walk in the steps of Christ."

"What has brought that to mind?"

Theodulf's eyes twinkled as he looked at André. "I remember teaching in one of the schools we had established just outside of Orleans. Our lesson in Scripture was from Matthew's Gospel about the moment Jesus entered Jerusalem, triumphantly, as a king, just days before he was betrayed, accused, humiliated, and crucified. I asked the students in the room that day—that chilly, drafty room—what about the passage struck them the most. And I got the most unusual, and helpful, reply."

André bowed his head. He knew this story was meant for him as much as for Theodulf's memory.

"A boy of about fourteen years of age said, 'Yes, it seems very painful that so many people cheered Him and called Hosanna that Sunday, and then they implored Pilate to crucify Jesus that coming Friday.' I looked straight at the lad and asked, 'What lesson might we draw from this?' And what do you think he said?"

André let his mind go back to that classroom so many years ago...

"'' ... that we follow in Jesus' steps,''' André reflected, "'and we must be prepared for praise and regard to be fleeting and find hardship and humiliation to mark the road we walk.'''

Theodulf cocked his head, the memory coming full circle in that room. "So spoke the student, who became in that moment, an unwitting teacher."

"In Rebrechien," André added.

"Yes, in the Eglise Notre Dame, André. You were that child who saw that in the story of Christ and pressed it into my life. Did you ever imagine that what you offered that day would be the truth that inspired me to live faithfully now in my exile?"

"I am humbled, Your Grace, that you believe so," André replied, "but I am still puzzled. How does that inspire you now?"

Pushing himself gingerly from the chair, Theodulf wobbled over to the table against the wall, upon which several sheaves of paper lay, covered with a flowery yet firm script. Bringing the papers back, he placed them in André's hands and nodded for him to read what was before him.

"It looks like poetry, Your Grace," André mentioned as he read the verse, "but you are telling a story."

"The story of Christ entering Jerusalem that first Palm Sunday, glorified then only to be cursed later," Theodulf agreed. "Your answer, André, has led to this, a song in which we see that to follow the Lord of Glory is to go the way of the Cross, so that we might give Him praise and honor!"

"This is incredible, Your Grace," André replied. "I do hope that you offer this to the abbot that we might chant it."

"You know, André, I was going to do just that, given that Palm Sunday is approaching soon. This would make a wonderful hymn. But as I now have before me the one whose answer inspired these words; I have something to ask you."

"Which is?"

"Might we chant this together, the two of us, here, right now?"

His eyes moistening, André nodded his joyful agreement. Sharing the pages with Theodulf, the two of them joined together with low, cheerful, jubilant voices, and sang forth in the flickering candlelight:

"All glory, laud, and honor to thee, Redeemer King,
To whom the lips of children made sweet hosannas ring
Thou art the King of Israel, Thou David's royal Son
Who in the Lord's name comest, the King and Blessed One!
The company of angels are praising Thee on high

And mortal men and all things created make reply.
The people of the Hebrews with palms before Thee went,
Our praise and love and anthems before Thee we present.
To Thee, before Thy passion, they sang their hymns of praise
To Thee, now high exalted, our melody we raise
Thou didst accept their praises! Accept the love we bring,
Who in all good delightest, Thou good and gracious King!"[2]

THEODULF traveled from southern France to accept the summons of Holy Roman Emperor Charlemagne to be the Bishop of Orleans. Working with the court deacon, Alcuin, Theodulf used his skill and intellect to found schools in many towns, free of charge for the education of poor and wealthy alike. A faithful church leader, Theodulf continued much of the revival of learning in the Carolingian Renaissance throughout the Holy Roman Empire, preserving much wisdom and knowledge for future generations. Wrongly accused of treason by King Louis the Pious, Theodulf was removed as bishop and exiled to Angers. Considering his humiliation to mirror somewhat the hardship of Christ, there he penned the great Palm Sunday hymn, "All Glory, Laud, and Honor", before dying two years later in 821.

---

2. https://christianhistoryinstitute.org/incontext/article/all-glory-laud-and-honor/

ANSELM

1096, Canterbury, England

A stiff breeze swirled the autumn leaves over the feet of the archbishop as he stepped onto the main path that hugged the River Stour. Having left Canterbury Cathedral only minutes before, Anselm shuffled along the road, alone with his thoughts and the clack-clack of his walking stick. He looked back with pride at the cathedral, its rebuilding finished less than a quarter-century before, and then continued on. Judging from the position of the setting sun, he was likely late to the dinner. That wasn't what pricked at his heart. The real question was why he had been invited. James Yohe had proven himself to be one of the learned people in the city and an able printer and binder of books, in spite of the expense of doing so. He and his wife Anne had invited Anselm to a sumptuous feast in their dwelling. When James wants you for food, he wants to talk, thought Anselm. The archbishop shook his head. He was more comfortable when the Yohe patriarch was silent or reserved; when James became talkative was when Anselm grew anxious.

He watched the gentle flow of the river as he trudged onward, and seeing the Sturgeon Inn about two hundred paces ahead, Anselm looked for the Yohes' large home on the right off the lane. Making it to the door, he rapped three times and Anne almost immediately answered.

"Your Grace, God bless you!" she said while bowing low. "Please come in. The fish and potatoes are on the table and we are ready for you to bless the meal."

"Thank you, dear Anne," Anselm acknowledged her kindness, stepping through the door still mystified by the invitation.

"That was a grand meal, m'lady," chortled James to his wife as he threw some sweet wood chips into the fire. Anselm was as glad for the warmth as he was for James' present jovial behavior. Setting his mug of cider in front of him, Anselm pulled himself forward to the table as Anne allowed their children, George and Jane to be excused.

"They are fine children," Anselm complimented, knowing the remark would still invoke memories of the four children the Yohes had lost to illness in their infancy.

"Indeed they are," Anne agreed, "and we are grateful to God."

"Speaking of which," James said as he roughly sat down. "This issue of God. I know you must be wondering why the invitation to dinner. Yes, Your Grace, you deserve it, but I admit I had a slightly selfish motive."

Anselm smiled. "I admit I guessed that. Given that you are my publisher, it wouldn't have to do with the book, would it?"

James cackled and looked at his wife, reaching over and touching her hand. "Naïve men do not become archbishops, that is for certain. Yes, Your Grace, I took publisher's liberty to read your book and as I worked through it, it unearthed several questions. Respectful ones, I hope, Your Grace, but questions nonetheless."

"First, James, questions are welcomed. Our Lord Jesus taught mainly through the use of questions. And secondly to both of you, while I am your archbishop, I am also your friend. No need to call me 'Your Grace' over dinner. 'Anselm' will do."

The Yohes looked grateful. "Very well, Anselm," Anne replied, "although that will take some getting used to."

"But there is the matter of questions," Anselm prodded. "And I am surprised at your labor in reading it. It is meant for churchmen's clarification."

"I picked up enough Latin in my younger years to facilitate a rough understanding. My uncle was a parish priest who was very well read and I picked up even more than he realized. As far as my questions, it has more to do with the very premise of your work."

Anne held her husband's hand. "For him, it began with the very title itself. *Why God Man*?"

"You had some differences with my views?" Anselm asked James, who had edged away from the table toward the warmth of the fire.

"Not so much the case you made, Your Gr—ah, Anselm," he muttered. "I had questions regarding why it was necessary. You speak at length that God in Christ came to earth in human flesh. But could not He have come as a human and become God instead? Why does the order matter?"

"There are other reasons, to be honest, Anselm," Anne added. "In spite of God's blessings upon our family, losing four children has been difficult to bear. We both know this is not unusual. Families throughout our town suffer the loss of little children. I think what you must hear is a cry of the heart: If Jesus is God who became man, and He came into our world to suffer and die, we are still left with our own suffering. Many people are. What then?"

Anselm spread his hands on the table. "Are you both saying that there are others besides you who have questions like these?"

"A fair number," James replied. "I am not saying that they would fill the cathedral, Anselm, but if we met together, the chapel on the eastern end, just behind the presbytery, would be a snug room indeed. I am sorry to bring this up. It seems as if we are questioning you as our archbishop. But we do have honest questions."

"No, I understand, James," said Anselm when a thought occurred to him. "In that case, James, Anne, could you send word to others who bear your burden for truth? Could you gather them together in the chapel and I will hear them out?"

James and Anne looked at each other. "We can," Anne blurted out. "When?"

"Four days from now," Anselm replied. "Monday after evening prayers. And you are right, James. The chapel will be a perfect place."

That following Monday what amazed James and Anne, as the bodies in the chapel raised the warmth considerably, was that the debate never got heated. Anselm was the picture of calm and ease. Question after question poured out of the mouths of several townspeople, and Anselm listened and answered each one with kindness and authority. Not everyone, Anselm knew, had read his book, but the stories and rumors of it were surprisingly accurate. Rather than being distressed about gossip, he was grateful for the profound interest in the Scriptures from his townsfolk.

A stocky innkeeper stepped forward with the confidence and swagger with which he served visitors and regulars at the Sturgeon Inn. "Your Grace," he asked in his choppy, Saxon accent, "I tend to be a simple man, given to simple, straightforward ways. For years we gather in church to hear the prayers and receive the sacrament of Eucharist at your hands and the hands of the priests. We pray for the forgiveness of our sins. I am not so much in disagreement with you about what it is said you wrote. I wonder if it is another teaching to lay on top of the simple way we already follow. To borrow from your title, I ask why it is necessary to believe that God became man?"

"Meaning why Jesus Christ?" Anselm clarified.

"We all take it as a given that Jesus was born, lived, died, and rose again," the innkeeper continued.

"What he means," said a woman seated nearby, "is why do we need Jesus to come as man? Why in that manner?"

Anselm nodded. "Let me ask this question of all here," Anselm replied winsomely. "What advantage might the arrival of Christ as the God-Man be for us?"

"To bring us to heaven?" a stableman piped up, waving his hands toughened by horse-keeping and horseshoe repair.

"Yes, there is that," Anselm agreed, pointing to the gatekeeper. "What else?"

"That sin does not hold us prisoner forever," the gatekeeper offered.

"Yes!" Anselm encouraged them. "Let us take that matter raised earlier. We are sinners, plunged into rebellion and corruption and separated from God. Yet God comes to us in the person of His Son, Jesus, who according to the apostle Paul was equal to God the Father but willingly gave up that exaltation to be born. Born as what?"

"As one of us," the stableman answered.

"As one of us...what? What are we? What is our burden?"

"Sin," the gatekeeper replied, "separation from God."

"And let us consider what advantage that might bring us, good people," Anselm continued. "We who are brought low by our sin, can we right ourselves?"

"Is that what baptism, the Eucharist, and penance are for?" asked James.

"The sacraments are for the people of God," Anselm redirected, "but how can we become the people of God if wrecked by the sin that divides us from the Almighty? Is the debt we owe like that of a peasant or serf to his lord? Like a noble to his king? Can we make up the debt from the wealth of our action and good works?"

A widow spoke up, "We cannot pay what we owe to God as our King."

Anselm added, “Remember in the Scriptures, the apostle Paul tells us that we are by nature children of wrath. We cannot make this payment by ourselves.”

“Then why does God not offer forgiveness immediately?” the innkeeper calmly inquired. “Why does that require the entry of the Lord Christ into our world? If God is love, why does he not show it by forgiveness?”

“A wise question,” Anselm responded, pivoting in his direction. “And he might, if not for the fact that God is a God of justice, and he cannot deny justice unless he denies himself. So, payment must be made.”

“But you yourself said we cannot!” exclaimed another.

“Indeed, we cannot.”

“But we must make payment for sin.”

“Indeed, we are responsible as peasants of sin to our Lord of glory.”

Another man put his face in his hands. “This is dreadful, and I never realized it. We cannot make restitution to God, and yet we must?”

Anselm smiled, walked toward the man, and removed his hands from his face. “That is not dreadful news, Tom. Nor let any man or woman think that. It is the best news of all!”

“The best news?” the innkeeper scoffed. “How?”

“In Christ, both our most pressing quandaries are met in His life and sacrifice,” Anselm’s voice rang joyfully. “As Christ is God, he is able to make payment. We are unable to live in holy perfection as God demands, so He meets His own demands in His holy life. And as man, He takes our place and dies the death we deserve. We are unable to atone for our evil, yet we are responsible to make amends. In Christ, God who became man, we are rescued indeed.”

The crowd erupted into joyful cheer and calls at Anselm’s response. He might have ended the assembly then and there if not for seeing two troubled souls within the throng.

James and Anne.

Anselm raised his hands for quiet and then beckoned the Yohes forward. They were ten feet away when he said, "I know your heart has questions that my previous words could not mend. But you are among friends in this place, James and Anne. We can listen to your heart even now."

James could hardly speak. Anne merely squeezed her husband's hand and looked at Anselm, saying, "You know of our inquiry, Your Grace. And we know you will not run from it. And we agree with all you have said tonight of why Jesus came. Our question is not why the God-Man came. It is why He allowed our little ones to die so soon." And her voice died in her many tears.

It was then that Anselm, in a way that none expected the archbishop to act, reached forth and embraced both James and Anne, pulling them in and holding them tightly. There, in a voice they all could hear, he said, "Dear ones, grief is harsh and unanswerable. I could say there are no words but there is a resurrection, and while true, that does not close your wounds. All I can say is that the Jesus who lived among us knows your pain and so much more. He came among us to receive our pain so He might be within you as you grieve. Losing our children is a horror indescribable. All I can offer is this: That the Holy Spirit sustained your infants' lives on earth. That when each of them died, the first person to cry for them was God our Father Himself. And when they entered heaven, Jesus, God who became man, was the one who stretched forth His arms and embraced them more tightly than I embrace you now."

The chapel was completely silent, no faces therein without tears. It was as if time had stopped in a moment of holy joy.

"Thank you," James whispered.

"Yes," Anne added, "and that being true, who else do we have to follow except Christ Himself?"

The ministry of **ANSELM** (born in Italy in 1033) spanned many turbulent years, especially after he was chosen in 1093 to succeed his mentor Lanfranc as the archbishop of Canterbury in England. His scholarly mind and pastoral heart oversaw the days that followed the Norman conquest of England, and his spiritual direction aimed to help priests and laypeople both to have a credible understanding of the Christian faith within a life of holiness. Along with his book *Why God Man?*[1], which spelled out his biblical understanding of Jesus' substitution for us on the Cross to atone for our sin, Anselm involved himself in other wide-ranging pursuits. He crafted an argument for the existence of God, and he defended the rights of the Church to name its leaders instead of allowing the king to do so. Dying in 1109, Anselm never swerved from his firm conviction that faith led to the flourishing of wisdom, or as he said, "I do not seek to understand that I may believe, but I believe so that I may understand."

---

1. It's important to note that Anselm's books took a great deal of time and energy to print. This was years before Johannes Gutenberg would invent the movable type printing press. In Anselm's day, one would have to carve the book's contents on wooden blocks page by page, and this was a long and labor-intensive activity. The other alternative would be for the books to be copied and re-copied by hand in the many monasteries throughout Europe, where monks would diligently and painstakingly re-produce the manuscripts of great writers and thinkers."

GREAT BRITAIN
CANTERBURY
CARDIFF
LONDON
PARIS

BERNARD OF CLAIRVAUX

1120, Vallée d'Absinthe, France

The door creaked loudly as it opened into the courtyard. Blinking in the brightness of the sun on this late summer day, Francois held the heavy wooden slab open as his master, the abbot, walked through the doorway with halting steps, his body, more worn and stooped than that of a normal thirty-year old.

He is wearing himself out, thin and tired, with no true rest for his mind, body, or soul, thought Francois, knowing that to raise these matters with Bernard would be pointless.

The stream of monks that followed numbered some twenty men, representing little more than a tenth of the residents at the Clairvaux Abbey. In true Benedictine fashion, Bernard had ordered the majority of monks to remain in their rhythm of prayer and work, while bringing the ones he believed absolutely necessary for a show of solidarity. Francois knew many of the residents in the courtyard now would say little, if anything, during the coming confrontation, but Bernard would use it to his advantage.

"Francois," Bernard rasped, his white cuccula[1] robe hanging loosely over his habit that concealed his brittle body, "I could not see in the darkness of the chapel when we left. Is William St. Thierry with us?"

"Yes, Father," Francois smiled, "I made sure you are not without your legal champion." He turned to his right, for the abbey door had swung open, and a line of black-robed monks strode through it into the middle of the courtyard.

1. A hooded robe.

"The welcome of your abbey is notable, Abbot Bernard," called out Pons de Melgueil, the abbot of Cluny Abbey, "and though not all are arrayed before us, I am certain your entire community bids us welcome."

Bernard's eyes glinted at the abbot, and his mind noted the sarcasm through the apparently warm gratitude. Stepping forward with a slight limp, he replied, "Thank you, most reverend Father Pons, for your kind words. I am grateful to see you brought wise counsel with you, as well." He nodded toward the venerable and soft-eyed Peter Montboissier to the abbot's right.

"I would not miss the chance to come to Clairvaux, good Abbot Bernard," Peter bowed. "And we are grateful you will host our overnight stay."

"Receive another as you would receive Christ," Bernard answered, feeling his knees give way a bit and thankful for Francois' grip on his arm. "That is the Benedictine way. The spirit that binds us together, in fact. And perhaps this is the day we can place the darkness aside and find some common ground as brothers in Christ?"

"Then you will do well to let us speak," said William St. Thierry, moving forward into their midst, "with chosen monks from each side brought as witnesses?"

"This was not part of the agreement," snarled Pons, "but we were to speak, the two of us face to face. Abbot Bernard and myself. The disagreement is between us."

"I will not deny that hostility exists," Bernard said sharply, "but it is one that has overwhelmed Clairvaux and your community at Cluny. These problems might have arisen between individuals, but they engulf all of us who desire to be conformed to the image of Christ. I have William, you have the respected Peter. I say we could also bring forth three monks from each side to hear out these charges and work through them together."

Seeing he would get nowhere until Bernard was the happy host, Pons shook his head and turned to three monks behind him, waving. "You three! Come forth!"

Bernard pressed his fingers into Francois' arm, his frailty frightening for a man of only thirty years of age. "Francois," he rasped, "would you be good enough to signal two others forward to join with us?"

"With a good will, Father," he replied, waving two men forward until the circle of ten was complete. The cluster of bodies in the center of the courtyard faced each other like opposing sides before a battle.

Pons smiled, his expression kind but firm as he began, "Kind Father Bernard, we have come in person to discuss these matters. I believe that no one doubts your sincerity in the establishment of your house here at Clairvaux. Nor could we deny the power of the Holy Spirit that influences men to come and serve Christ here under the banner of the Benedictine order. Our issues are not with those matters, but with the substance of your vision for this abbey, and your insinuation that we are inferior to your discipline and diligence here at Clairvaux!"

Bernard knew better, but he allowed William to speak first in reply. "Is this the assessment of all of you from Cluny?"

One of the Cluny monks spoke. "May we give Abbot Bernard a chance to express what has been meant, rather than what we might intend to hear. Abbot Pons, it is what we would want were we accused of something."

The Cluny abbot looked at the monk with sudden disappointment but gathered himself together and looked back at Bernard. "My friend Father Bernard, the differences between us are greater than just the white robes of your monks and the black robes of mine. The discipline of our order, for both our abbeys, goes all the way back to Benedict himself. But there is a distinction between discipline and backbreaking rigidity. One has value, the other grants frustration in the end."

Bernard gestured William to respond. "Are you certain," the lawyer inquired, "that you are speaking wisely? Have you lived even a week here to know what our community is like?"

"The reports of Robert de Chatillon are enough to convince me," Pons replied.

"They convince you because he is my cousin," Bernard said, wincing at the sudden pain in his ribs, "and you practically stole him from this abbey, offering him an easier life within your walls at Cluny."

"That's a lie!" Pons shot back.

Francois stepped forward. "You dare accuse our abbot of falsehood?"

"Francois," Bernard interrupted, "address our guests as if they were Christ Himself." He looked at Pons. "But what of it? Is our community unnecessarily stringent? Do we require more of these monks than they can give?"

"I'd remind you," added Pons, "that I have already said your labor is backbreaking. As you yourself said, Bernard, stringent!"

"Wouldn't the better path be to ask the monks here," replied one of the Clairvaux monks, "if the labor is too rigid and difficult? And, speaking for all of us, I'd say the answer to that would be a resounding 'no.'"

"To speak to that matter," Bernard said gently, "what we do within the walls of Clairvaux is nothing more than what Benedict himself set forth with his Rule. We have the scriptorium here for copying of manuscripts, but we also build and repair areas of the abbey, fashion pumps and storage wells for water, make wine and ale, grow our vegetables for our meals so that we might be self-sufficient, and make chairs and tables for our use and that of the nearby townspeople. This is nothing more than a resurrection of the principles and demands that Benedict himself made when he founded his monasteries. Your monks at Cluny function as scholastics and woodworkers; you do well! But we do not limit ourselves to those ventures! We liberate our monks from idleness and unleash them toward the service to God for which they took vows."

"We must wisely use the time that is granted to us." Pons responded.

"The abbot speaks the truth," one of Pons' monks added forcefully.

Bernard looked at the Cluny monks across from him. "Help me, Father," he prayed. "What wisdom can I give them?" And then the reply came, as clear as a bell. "Calm yourself. I am with you."

Looking at Pons, Bernard bowed, the effort cracking his back loudly. "Good Father, we would go in circular fashion this entire day over the point of our schedules. You are entirely right to desire the service of God above all else. I desire the ones in my charge to see it as taking on a yoke, the weight of which shall make them strong. We are populating new abbeys throughout France. The rate at which we do so appears rapid. It is not done to humiliate your abbey or to render it insignificant."

Bernard thought that Pons had not anticipated that reply. Bernard continued, "I simply wish us to recall what it means to serve Christ in the abbey. Ora et labora, as our master Benedict said. We are both communities of labor. We are both communities of prayer. That is beyond dispute."

"And yet we are having a dispute at the moment," a Cluny monk broke in with considerable audacity.

"Quiet, my son!" Pons exclaimed to his defender.

"Refrain yourselves, all of you," Peter added, "and let us hear out our friend Father Bernard."

Ever since his brief, silent prayer to God, Bernard had sensed a gradual strengthening of his voice, spirit, and bones. Standing straight, he continued. "We take our vision, not from the need to fill time and keep from idleness, as important as that may be. We draw our vision for serving Christ from the very nature of Christ Himself, His humility, His tender nature, and His willingness to suffer. We are companions on the journey which He walked! Jesus is the Son of Man, pouring out His very sweat and blood as He lived among us, was despised and rejected by others, and was crucified in agony and brutality. He is our Sacred Head, now wounded![2] The very thought of Him should fill our hearts with sweetness and fire, and His Holy Spirit should be the very breath of our lungs! I ask all of us assembled here, that if what we see about our Lord Jesus Christ does not inspire us to pursue Him with every heartbeat, if what we believe about our Saviour's suffering does not inspire us to suffer as well, and if His death does not press upon us the need to live unselfishly, then what indeed are we proclaiming by our lives within abbey walls?"

It was clear that both Pons and Peter were shaken by Bernard's passionate words. Indeed, many among the black-robed monks murmured in acknowledgement. One young monk tugged on Peter's robe and sighed, "It is much to ask."

"We have been given more than we can imagine," Peter replied, his eyes to the ground, "and so much might be required."

Pons stood in front of Bernard. "Do you really believe that unceasing rigor will bring life to an abbey?"

"The pursuit is not in rigor for rigor's sake, Abbot Pons," Bernard croaked, "but in the pursuit of Christ and the bold strides we make upon the path He walked. Even the apostle Paul told the Colossians that he rejoiced...he rejoiced in his sufferings, he found magnificence in the trials he faced

2. This refers to Bernard's hymn, 'O Sacred Head, Now Wounded' referring to Jesus as our Savior who died on our behalf.

because they filled up what he said needed to be continued... what the sufferings of Christ had begun, it is our privilege, for the sake of His Church, to continue them."

Pons looked directly at Bernard. "You will take your stand here, unmoved?"

"My dear Father," Bernard replied, "why do you fear what we have done here at Clairvaux? Believe me when I tell you that your community at Cluny will continue. I dearly love your monks at Cluny as much as I love the brothers of any order in any place. More than anything, could we part on that accord? But first, please, stay for a morsel to eat, and then join us for labor and prayers."

Pons couldn't speak, merely touching Bernard on the arm and then turning back to the Cluny monks. Peter clasped Bernard's hand while William supported the abbot's balance.

"Father Bernard," Peter said, "thank you for that. I know that convincing Abbot Pons will not come immediately. He loves the abbey at Cluny as I do, and there is considerable rumor that he will be designated elsewhere."

"And will you take his place?" asked Bernard.

"It is entirely likely," Peter allowed, "and if so, you have given me much to ponder."

It was as Peter ended his sentence that the two men looked aside and saw a magnificent sight, the monks of Clairvaux beckoning their Cluny counterparts toward them and bidding them welcome. On the air came a sound, a sweet sound and a most beautiful one.

"Have they begun prayers here and now?" Peter asked, grinning.

"A poem of mine," Bernard chuckled, shuffling toward the growing, happy crowd of monks, "that they set to music."

He and Peter made their way toward the monks, who chanted forth.

"Jesus, Thou Joy of loving hearts, Thou Fount of Life,
Thou Light of men,
From fullest bliss that earth imparts we turn unfilled to
Thee again.
We taste Thee, O Thou Living Bread, and long to feast
upon Thee still.
We drink of Thee, O Fountainhead and thirst our souls
from Thee to fill.
O Jesus, ever with us stay—Make all our moments calm
and bright.
Chase the dark night of sin away—Shed over us Thy
holy light."[3]

Although this story is likely a fictional one, it reflects the manner in which **BERNARD**[4] answered the charges against him by the leaders of Cluny Abbey in 1119-20. Penning a winsome yet firm letter, Bernard made clear that the strict discipline of his abbey at Clairvaux, of which he became abbot at the age of twenty-five in 1115, was designed to reflect the passion and determination of the Christian life. In time, this brought about a wave of reform through Benedictine monasticism in western Europe, mainly through Cluny Abbey, where Peter the Venerable eventually became abbot. Bernard busied himself in many other pursuits, urging participation in the Second Crusade and speaking against heretics who denied the atonement of Jesus Christ. A poet who wrote the words to many hymns we use today—including "O Sacred Head, Now Wounded", Bernard remained abbot of Clairvaux until his death there in 1153.

---

3. https://hymnary.org/text/jesus_thou_joy_of_loving_hearts
4. Bernard's monasteries became a new religious order, the Cistercian Order.

FACT FILES

The Crusades

Perhaps you have gone on a vacation or holiday far away from your home. Imagine being so filled with expectation about the fun you will have that you could almost burst. Then every mile, every part of the journey becomes laden with hardship and bewilderment. The holiday is nothing like what it seemed at first. I hope you haven't had this experience, but whether you have or haven't, it's a bit like what happened in the Crusades.

In 1094, the Byzantine emperor Alexius Comnenus I sent a desperate communication to Pope Urban II. The Seljuk Turks, who had taken over the leadership of the Muslim world, were overwhelming the territories that were on the road to Constantinople and the center of the Byzantine Empire. Urban considered Alexius' request for military help, but his shrewd mind was thinking of other possibilities. For years, Christians from western Europe had (when able) made pilgrimages to the Holy Land of Israel, with a special focus on Jerusalem. To go and experience the places of Jesus' life and death was considered a major part of a Christian's life. The Church encouraged pilgrimages as a way of receiving God's special blessings of grace in their lives. What made these pilgrimages increasingly difficult was the presence of the Seljuk Turks in that region. The hostility and brutality of Seljuk raiders toward the traveling Christians provoked outrage amongst the Catholic leadership. Seizing a chance to marry Alexius' plea for action with a military push to conquer new lands, Urban II took action decisively.

At a council in Clermont, France in November 1095, Urban preached a sermon to a crowd of priests, knights, and nobles which proved highly effective. He called for a great army of Christians to march from western Europe to the Holy Land. The order was simple: Make it possible for pilgrims to reach their destinations by wrenching control of the Holy Land from the Muslims. The assembled congregation went wild, screaming "God wills it! God wills it!", and armies began to assemble for departure throughout European lands. Ensuring that more warriors would take up the sword, Urban made a sweeping promise: If a soldier died while serving on a crusade, God would grant him full forgiveness of all sins and eternal life in heaven.

Taking the name crusaders (from the Latin "crux", meaning "cross"), the newly-minted soldiers took off for Palestine with great enthusiasm and fervor. Sincerely wanting to free the land of Christ from the Seljuk Turks, the Crusaders faced a long journey on the First Crusade (1096-1099), difficult battles (they barely took Antioch from the Turks, aided by the frenzy of allegedly having seen a vision of a lance in the sky), and disease. A campaign that began with a mighty force of many tens of thousands saw the army dwindle to a much smaller remnant by the time they reached the gates of Jerusalem. This proved to be plenty, however, as the Turks had spent so much energy fighting each other in petty squabbles they were hardly unified against the Crusaders. In June 1099, after besieging Jerusalem for six weeks, the Crusaders breached the walls and invaded the city. Once inside, they were hardly the models of Christian virtues, committing unspeakable acts and slaughter against the Muslim and Jewish inhabitants of the city, including women and children.

At this point, the Crusades took on a different look. Once having secured their victory, many Crusaders desired to stay in the Holy Land, building kingdoms where the knights would settle and own farmed estates. The wealth created by a number of these ventures began to shift the focus of many crusaders from a pilgrimage to free the Holy Land to an opportunity to live well in the Holy Land. Many of what were called "Latin kingdoms" sprang up throughout Palestine: Lesser Armenia, Antioch, Edessa, and Tripoli, among others. The chief kingdom, though, was centered around Jerusalem, where Godfrey de Bouillon reigned as the first of many kings and Christians submitted to a new Catholic archbishop.

Although this arrangement held for a while, the Muslims were not going to fade away quietly. In 1144, Seljuk Turks overran the kingdom of Edessa, threatening to undo what the Crusaders had won half a century before. In France, Bernard of Clairvaux (whom we've already encountered) grew indignant that Christians should cede any ground in the Middle East, and in 1147 he preached the necessity of a Second Crusade to recapture the lost territory, and another flood of knights—led by the French king Louis VII and the Holy Roman Emperor Conrad III—marched toward the Holy Land. This time the results were not in the Christians' favor. Disease, lack of food, and a failed attack on Damascus doomed the crusaders' efforts, and they marched home leaving Edessa in Muslim hands. Upon their return, Bernard—normally the model of charity and kindness—berated them for their failure, claiming their defeat was punishment for their vile sins against Christ. It was a sad explosion of temper from an ordinarily sweet and gentle monk.

Although the Seljuk Turks had experienced their own internal divisions, all they required was a powerful, charismatic leader to unite them to victory, and when Saladin was crowned Sultan of Egypt in 1174, the Turks had the man who would lead them to triumph. The next year, Saladin conquered all of Egypt; seven years after that, he crushed the northern Crusader kingdoms in Syria and had surrounded the kingdom of Jerusalem in a pincer-like fashion. In 1187, he finally took Jerusalem, ending the Crusaders' eighty-eight-year rule there and provoking the Third Crusade in response. The effort was plagued by disaster and divisions amongst its leaders. King Richard (the Lionheart) of England constantly bickered with King When? In the past? Philip Augustus of France, and Holy Roman Emperor Frederick Barbarossa drowned en route to Jerusalem. In spite of intense fighting, the Crusaders could not recapture Jerusalem. However, as an expression of admiration toward Richard, Saladin granted the Crusaders an area of land at Acre, a port city on the Mediterranean Sea, and guaranteed pilgrim access to Jerusalem. It should be noted that the Jews in Jerusalem were somewhat relieved by Saladin's victory, as he treated them noticeably better than the Crusaders had.

Subsequent crusades never reached the high-water mark the Crusaders had enjoyed in 1099. Pope Innocent III, determined to regain the Holy Land, ordered the Fourth Crusade in 1202, but the French force that went was stranded in Constantinople and ended up looting and destroying much of the city. As we'll encounter later, Francis of Assisi preached to the Sultan Al-Kamil in 1219 in the Fifth Crusade. However, this effort ended in disaster for the Crusaders as Al-Kamil retreated to Cairo and, when the Crusaders followed his army, he ordered the dams on the Nile opened, stopping their advance and ensuring Muslim victory after a subsequent attack.

Frederick II was able to negotiate with the Turks to become king in Jerusalem after the Sixth Crusade, but the vigor and victory of past campaigns was beginning to fade. A Children's Crusade of boys and girls, ordered in the misguided belief that the pure and innocent of heart would win out over the Turks, ended in disaster as many children either got lost, enslaved, died of disease, or were killed on the way to the Holy Land. Finally, even the Crusader city of Acre could not hold out against Seljuk attacks, and in 1291 it fell to Muslim forces, ending a nearly two-hundred-year conflict with disaster.

Although the Crusades were a frustrating experience, it changed the world and the Church in various ways. First, the warring activity gave rise to several military monastic orders, which operated on a code of chivalry to protect the weak and swore obedience to the Pope. Such groups included the Knights of St. John (also known as the Hospitallers) who tended sick and wounded pilgrims; the Knights Templar whose wealth and warring influence spread from the Jerusalem temple site into Europe; and the Teutonic (Germanic) Knights who sought to conquer other kingdoms in eastern Europe.

The Crusades also strengthened the influence and impact of the papacy. Popes such as Urban II and Innocent III were able to use the force of their personality to both call for and direct different crusades. To fund these expeditions, popes discovered that the sale of indulgences could provide needed money to pay for military efforts. Indulgences were notices offered to people by which, if they paid a certain amount of money, the purchaser would receive a spiritual gift of grace, such as shortened time in purgatory—taught by the Catholic Church as a place of purging after death from unforgiven sins before entering heaven. Martin Luther later attacked their usage at the dawn of the Protestant Reformation 300 years later.

In the meantime, the noble class in Europe was financially weakened, and families devastated by these losses had difficulty adjusting to this "new normal." With the social layers below them in tatters, kings and queens gathered more power to themselves throughout western Europe. In addition, the Crusades had caused even more division between western and eastern Christians, especially after the looting of Constantinople during the Fourth Crusade. And simmering hostility remained between Christians and Muslims after the conflicts, an opposition that is evident in many ways to the present day. However, there were some avenues that led to a greater awakening between the two sides. Christians in the Holy Land noticed that Muslim scholars had translated many classic works such as those of Plato and Aristotle as some had already noticed in Muslim Spain. This led to some extended conversation between the two groups, and the Christians who returned home with documents and books paved the way for the continued flowering of knowledge, the rise of more universities throughout Europe, and the increased commerce of both goods and ideas between East and West.

PETER WALDO

1185, near Roaschia, Italy

With the sound of scraping metal, shuffling feet, and angry voices drawing ever nearer, the huddled refugees pressed themselves into the darkest crevices of the cave. As agreed, many of the mothers with babies were the furthest back. The theory was, Pierre reasoned, that if they could gather near one of the springs in the rear, any running water could drown out the cries of children that might give them away. It ran significant risk, some of his fellow escapees told him, that soldiers would follow the sound of water if they were thirsty enough in these high mountains and find the women and children nonetheless. However, this was the only plan that could work, although it remained fraught with danger as long as the papal warriors stalked around the mountain.

"Cursed mountain!" came a roar from the mouth of the cave, and a hand swept in and waved a torch a few feet inside the opening. Pierre crouched further down in the shadows, careful not to slip and give away his position or that of the dozens behind him in the dank, rocky chamber.

"See anyone?" came a surly question. "Or can we head west and deal with those miserable Cathars?"

"I thought I saw someone in there, sure," came the reply, "but perhaps the light's flicker made it seem so."

"Insane idea for people to live up in these cursed holes," the other snapped gruffly. "Ah well, all the same, if they want to spend their life on the run, they can make every attempt until they starve themselves in these mountains.

Better to head into the valley towns where the Cathar heretics walk about in broad daylight. At least we can tell His Holiness we tried." Sending a shrill whistle through his teeth, he then bellowed to what had to be the rest of the contingent. "All right, men. We have no time to waste in these rocks! Let's move out!"

So intent had Pierre been listening to the soldiers that he failed to notice his cousin Florian had silently moved right behind him, causing him a brief startle. "Peter!" Florian mouthed quietly. "Have they gone?"

Pierre frowned, irked at the use of his previous name. "They are going away, Florian," he replied, "but I think it wise if we remain still for another ten to fifteen minutes. That way we know they are gone."

He could sense that Florian was annoyed at the prospect of a further wait and increasing cramps and pains in the legs, but Pierre desired his people be safe rather than comfortable. The minutes trickled by slowly until Pierre finally stood, softly clapped Florian on the shoulder, and whispered, "Very well. Tell them they may move about and get something to eat. They will need their strength."

Florian nodded and crept back into the recesses of the cavern. Pierre waited a few moments and then he could hear the gradual shuffling of feet and the murmuring of parents and children. Looking back toward the mouth of the cave on the chance the intruders had returned, he stood guard until he saw Florian and his family standing next to him.

"You are certain they have left?" the wife implored, clutching her daughter's hand tightly as Florian placed his arm around their son.

Pierre nodded. "Quite sure," he answered. "And now that interruption is behind us, perhaps we can gather the children deep in the grotto for instruction."

Florian was incredulous. "You are wanting to go ahead and teach them, even though we were a hair's breadth from being discovered?"

"I did not come over hill and brook into these mountain crypts to stand watch at openings and offer passing blessings," Pierre uttered with a slight edge to his voice. "We have all suffered much when we were forced from home and scattered throughout these mountains. No, gather the children. God has raised me up to preach and so proclaim His wonders I must."

Florian's wife smoothed her daughter's dress. "Of course, we will. Florian, come with me and let's find the other children."

Florian nodded at Pierre and followed his wife through the nooks of the cave. Pierre watched them go, a lump forming in his throat as he thought of his words. *God has raised me up to preach and so proclaim his wonders I must.*

The call of Christ. The pain it brought. Pierre closed his eyes and remembered that day three years ago.

"Pierre Vaudoix," the bailiff thundered with great effort in the chapel. Priests swarmed around the interior of the Cathedrale Saint-Jean-Baptiste, practically buzzing like summer flies as the archbishop ascended to his throne. They might have been a loud bunch, thought Pierre, but once Archbishop John des Belles-Mains sat down, silence would reign, and only absolute respect of the cleric would give him a chance of being heard.

"Yes," replied Pierre. "I am Vaudoix."

"Further acknowledgements shall be made to His Grace," snarled the bailiff, as the archbishop shuffled his papers from the throne.

"Be within my heart and upon my tongue, Lord Jesus," Pierre prayed quietly, "and help me to receive the news with grace.

The archbishop clenched the papers in his left hand, hiked his elbow upon his knee, and stared down at Pierre, who was clad in a simple gray tunic with a black overcloak and breeches. "Master Vaudoix, you have been summoned here in the presence of God and of His holy shepherds, having given account of your convictions regarding the Church, sacraments, and Holy Scripture. We, your overseers, have generously allowed you to put forth in exacting fashion exactly what you believe and have led others to embrace."

"Begging your pardon, Your Grace," Pierre called out, taking a step closer to the throne from the floor below. "I am well aware of what I've shared before this court previously. The 'poor men' of Lyon who follow me in our tasks of ministry are well known. I would ask that you pass judgment now so that our Lord might direct me how I shall serve Him in the future."

Archbishop des Belles-Mains squeezed the papers more tightly, leaning toward Pierre and glaring at him. "Very well," he began. "We have concluded that your decision to take literally the command of Christ, to sell your possessions, give all your wealth away to the poor, and walk in the steps of Christ is most admirable."

"It is hardly admirable or worthy of praise," Pierre replied. "I merely journeyed where the rich young ruler would not go in Matthew's Gospel. I obeyed the word of Christ as a Christian should. Would a farmer refuse to plow his field? To obey the Lord is both duty and delight, but it is no more than what is required."

"Refusing to accept a compliment is hardly the picture of charity," grunted the archbishop.

"As is idolizing money within the house of God, Your Grace," Pierre spoke calmly, bringing splotches of red to the archbishop's cheeks.

"Silence!" snarled des Belles-Mains. "As to your other activities, the church that Christ has purchased with His own blood shall not abide by them. You implore that you and your fellow 'poor men' merely require the approval of heaven to preach to others, and that the approval of myself is unnecessary. This would be distressing on its own, but you have distanced yourself from God's grace with your other teachings."

"My instruction is rooted in the very Word of God," Pierre firmly replied, "while your teaching cannot be found in Holy Scripture!"

"They are warranted by the authority of the Church," the archbishop exploded, "and you have no standing to negotiate indecision or to flood the consciences of others with doubts regarding instruction on which the Church has already ruled! Pierre Vaudoix, you have prodded your followers to accept your view that the Holy Scriptures—not the Scriptures and the Church's declaration—are all that is necessary for the Christian life. You spit in the face of tradition by having the New Testament translated into the language of the people. You have repeatedly denied the existence of purgatory as a place of cleansing from sin before eternal life in Heaven! You deny the effectiveness of prayers for the dead or the purchase of indulgences! You offer the bread and cup in Holy Communion to your followers, although not even ordained as a priest, and you deny that the food and drink are turned into the body and blood of our Lord Jesus! And when we have patiently directed you to the authority of our Holy Father, the Pope, you deny that he has teaching authority over even the most common peasant preacher!"

"And I have repeatedly said," Pierre answered des Belles-Mains, "that if you can demonstrate from Holy Scripture—and not from the assumptions of the Church's whims—where I am in error, I will gladly revoke my views."

"To demand that of your overseers is not merely arrogant," the archbishop replied, "but also heretical."

Pushing himself up from the throne, he stomped down the steps and stood before Pierre face to face. "And because that is what you and your followers have proven to be, Lyon is your home no more. You are banished, never to return!"....

Pierre's thoughts returned to the present. The pain of that moment in his past lingered as the children entered the hollow of the cave. Pierre sat quietly on the flat-top boulder as the little ones found a seat in front of him. I will die one day, fading like the grass, Pierre reminded himself, but the Word of God planted in the souls of others will never die. He smiled kindly and rumpled the hair of the little girl closest to him.

"Good afternoon, children," he began.

"Good afternoon, Master Pierre," they chimed in unison.

He almost choked on tears. The last time they had met before being expelled from Lyon, he taught them in a park. His hair flowed down near his shoulders and his beard was nicely full. Now, he was forced to disguise himself by cropping his locks close to his scalp and shaving his beard, exposing the scar on his right cheek. The price of an outlaw, a price these children were paying by hiding in these caves with their families, while other families were scattered throughout towns and hamlets on either side of the mountains. Fugitives, all of them. Fugitives for Christ.

"In our time this morning, let us begin with prayer," Pierre continued. "Remember what our Lord Jesus said, when He said, 'Suffer the little children to come to me'. And one of the ways we might do that is in the privilege of prayer."

The little girl with rumpled hair spoke up with a quiet confidence, "Our Lord Jesus, we thank You for caves for keeping us safe. We thank you for Master Pierre who comes to this cave. And we thank you that You are with us in this cave, and that you call us your children. Amen."

"Amen," repeated the others, along with Pierre.

"Now, little ones," he started, "We have been reminded just now that the Lord Jesus is with us. There is a teaching which we would repeat when many of us were still in Lyon, and I want to talk about a part of it today with you, because it teaches us about who Jesus is. Are you ready?"

"We are," the children announced in unison.

"We would often confess in our worship that Christ is our life, and truth, and peace, and righteousness - our shepherd and advocate, our sacrifice and priest, who died for the salvation of all who should believe, and rose again for their justification. I want to speak with you briefly about how precious this is for each of you."

He cleared his throat and turned his hands palms up. "What do you think it means that Jesus is our advocate? What does that mean Jesus does for us?"

One of the boys excitedly raised his hand. "Is Jesus our lawyer?"

The children giggled as Pierre smiled and raised his hands to quiet them. "Well, that's an interesting comment, young man. Why do you say that?"

"Because my mother said that's what my father was in Lyon. He was an advocate for people, but I always heard he was a lawyer."

"In a way, that's true," Pierre replied encouragingly. "A lawyer advocates for people he is with in a court. That means he is on their side. He is for them. He defends them."

"So Jesus is for us and defends us?" asked a little girl with a freckled nose.

"Yes, indeed!" replied Pierre. "We believe that Jesus wants the best for us. When Jesus sees us, He sees us as His friends. He sees us as His dear family for which He would do anything! If someone fought against us, what do you think Jesus would do?"

"I think," Florian's son began, "that He would get between us and the enemy and fight back and not let us be harmed."

"He would fight back," Pierre agreed, with a trace of caution in his voice, "and we would never want harm to come to us, but what Jesus wants us to know is that whatever happens to us, we will never lose Him, and He will never lose us. Remember that great harm came to Jesus. Remember we say that He died for the salvation of all who should believe. And yet that harm to Jesus showed that He is for us and never stops defending us, His family!"

Florian's daughter spoke up gently. "Master Pierre, do you think we will leave this cave and go home?"

A lump formed in Pierre's throat. "I sincerely hope so, but we will have to see. Many people in many towns I meet ask me the same, both children and adults."

"I want to," chirped a little boy with raven black hair, "but I would rather be safe, and here with my family."

"Jesus wants me here," came a pippy voice from the end of the semicircle. Everyone turned, stunned that the tinny reply came from the youngest girl in the group. Pierre raised himself from the boulder and crept toward her, crouching in front of the child.

"Say that again, dear one?" he whispered kindly.

The girl, blinking her shimmering gray eyes, tapped her doll, resting in her lap, lightly with her fingers before looking at Pierre and then around at the others. "I just think Jesus wants me here. And maybe we will be safe and we will get to go back home. Maybe we will always stay here in the caves. Or maybe we will not be able to escape the soldiers." She looked down and sniffed. "But I say that Jesus died for me. And if He died for me and still loves me through His pain, I should be able to die and love Him through my pain."

Pierre could not believe his ears at the wisdom and grace from a little child. Reaching out, he took her hands. "I am so amazed at your faith, little one, so amazed!"

Florian's daughter moved closer and put her arm around her little friend. "I'll protect you, I really will! I won't let you die."

"It's okay," the girl replied, her lips quivering but her fingers tenting around her little doll in her lap. "If Jesus loves me and was willing to die for me, I want to love Him and be willing to die for Him."

Pierre could barely speak, and even if he could, his voice would be stopped by what happened. The children swarmed over him in a massive embrace. And then his tears flowed with those of the children.

"A brave little band of souls," he prayed. Oh, Lord Jesus, be with them in life. And be with them, if it be so, in death."

Pierre Vaudoix, known more commonly in history by his name in exile, **PETER WALDO**, became the leader of the movement known as the Waldensians, a group called "the reformers before the Reformation." Exiled by the Catholic Church from Lyon, France, Waldo and his followers followed the teachings of Christ in the New Testament, translated into their native Provencal language, and challenged many Church teachings they believed were absent in Scripture. Following Waldo's death in 1205, the Waldensians endured much persecution at the hands of the Church, with some soldiers throwing them off the cliffs above the mountain caves where they dwelt. But the desire to know God's Word and teach it clearly remained among the Waldensians, who truly sought Christ above all.

STEPHEN LANGTON

June 15, 1215, Runnymede, England

Of all days for it to have rained the night before, thought the archbishop as he took careful, steady strides over the wet grass, the moisture wetting the edges of his robes and soaking through his leather shoes. The sunlight glistened on the surface of the meadow. A gentle breeze brought the smell of fruit trees on the eastern wind, where anyone who sniffed the air would have relaxed upon experiencing the scent. However, Archbishop Stephen Langton's only reaction was to keep his head down as he walked toward the distant tent, grasping a collection of papers in his hand. The business of the day was at hand, and he knew what was at stake. So lost in his thoughts was he that his compatriot finally had to shout to break his distraction.

"Stephen!" His fellow cleric William Sainte-Mere practically bawled in his ear. "Remind me again why we are heading for the barons' canopy?"

Langton covered his mouth with his fist to stifle a cough before turning his head toward the bishop of London. "A matter of civilized decorum, William," he replied, the tone of his voice betraying weariness. "I want to secure that all the barons are properly registered upon the charter and that they are aware of the proceedings."

"You honestly believe the king will sign it?" William scoffed. "Even though you are the archbishop of Canterbury—the head over the Church of England!—the very idea this agreement will hold like a biblical covenant strikes me as absurd."

"I have every reason to believe that he will sign it and that it will hold," Stephen responded as they approached the fluttering banners of the barons. "I pray it will hold! I have drafted it so many times—over so many days."

As the archbishop of Canterbury drew open the red flap and entered the tent, more than twenty barons rose at Langton's presence and bowed slightly.

"Your Grace," came the voice of Richard de Clare. He stood gingerly, pained by his ride from Essex. "We are grateful for your company this morning."

Langton nodded and passed greetings around the circle. They were all here, including some of the most reputable barons in all of England: De Clare, Robert FitzWalter (all the way from Little Dunmow), his battle mate Saer de Quincy from Winchester, Geoffrey de Mandeville of Gloucester, Eustace de Vesci from Alnwick Castle near the Scottish border, and others. Langton swallowed hard. These were the men he had to convince, even before King John arrived momentarily. And even the king could end up surprising everyone.

"As you were, good nobles," Langton uttered in an attempt to put everyone at ease, "I am not the pope." The barons seated themselves after a brief, united bow. Gazing at the center of the tent, Langton saw a rough map of Runnymede Meadow on the table, with blocks and trinkets amassed on the surface, and a cold chill ran down his spine. Even in the hope of peace, he thought, they must prepare for the chance of war. Almighty God, please give me the strength of your Holy Spirit to prevent any bloodshed.

Looking around at the barons, Langton began, "We haven't much time before the king's entourage arrives here at Runnymede. And I know your armies have marched from distances that have tired them greatly, so I will make this abundantly clear. We shall aim for a peace this day, not a temporary truce or a respite from hostilities. A true peace with lasting circumstances."

"Begging your pardon, Your Grace," muttered de Quincy. "Your idealism speaks volumes to us, but what about King John's actions? Word has reached us that the archbishop of Dublin himself is in league with the king and has arranged for two ships to bring supplies and warriors to this land. John's lackey William Longuespee has contracted with the Welsh for four hundred bowmen. And John himself has gathered a host of mercenaries from Poitou in Aquitaine! Within the past two weeks, the king has been inspecting his troops near my estate. How are we to believe that this gathering isn't a ruse to set his strength upon us in pitched battle?"

The murmurs among the barons grew strong and rippled through the tent. Langton held up his hand.

"I will not defy the facts, de Quincy," he replied to the baron. "All you have said is true, so I shall not insult you. The king has been an industrious man. He has been a covert instigator. And he has charmed many into believing he rules from a position of strength. But there is more that is hidden than what you presently see. My good bishop William can attest to you that King John is not as confident as others have made you believe. Letters to Scarborough have demonstrated that our king has not paid his own servants and crossbowmen for months. He is facing financial ruin. Another consideration is this place itself. Runnymede is moist with rain and dew and will not serve as a quality ground for pitched battle. Then there is the matter of needing a respite. The king fights in France. While he smiles and charms in public, he rages and gnaws on sticks in private. I do not say this to demean him; I say it because it is the truth. King John is tired. And in his weariness, this realm needs a lasting peace."

"We all crave this peace, Archbishop Langton," said Geoffrey de Mandeville, "but we seek it from a king that stripped me of my estate and gave it to another. How can we act against such reckless, unchecked power?"

Langton nodded and approached the table. Sweeping his hand over it and knocking over the war-pieces on the map, he laid the parchment upon it. It was a long, intact length of sheepskin, dried, bleached, and scraped. Langton spread it out and beckoned the barons to stand around the table.

"Good barons," he replied to all while addressing de Mandeville's concerns, "you know of the demands you have made. You know how the king acts publicly even as I have reminded you of what is really true. What you see before you, in continuous Latin script, is the fruit of what I have sought to place before the king on behalf of this realm. If you object to what is before you, say so now, but not before you have read what might be negotiated."

Langton stood back, allowing the barons to crowd around the table and make sense of the document. Several minutes passed by, broken by harrumphs or questions, but as the hour went on it was clear that the words on the parchment were taking hold of the barons, in spite of what Langton judged to be a continuing air of skepticism.

Finally, the barons turned as one to Langton, who stood with Bishop William at his side. "Well, Your Grace," said Richard de Clare, "it is all a bit much to take in. The first thing I have to say is that we stand upon a moment where we take all people beyond the horizon of what is known about government. Ancient liberties restored, swift justice and credible witnesses demanded, protection of estates. You even state that no sheriff can deprive a peasant of their corn unless paid a fair price!"

"All of this," added de Quincy, "and you demand to restrict the authority of the king and to place a council of barons to observe that all the liberties of the realm are kept intact!"

"It is unheard of," marveled Eustace de Vesci, who had remained quite silent until now. "We are the ones who will check the king's power."

Geoffrey de Mandeville approached Langton. "And you believe the king will assent to this?"

"I do," Langton replied. "Even at the expense of my position."

"What do you mean?" de Mandeville asked.

"Did you not read the first words, Geoffrey?" de Clare replied from the table, pointing at the initial script upon the parchment. The barons gathered around again and beheld what he meant. "This," de Clare breathed. "Do you realize the enemies you might make, Your Grace, on both the throne of England and the throne of St. Peter's in Rome?"

All eyes turned to Langton, who bowed slightly, then lifted his head to meet their eyes.

"My barons," he said wearily, "I knew exactly what I was doing when I added that clause."

"It means we will only have a brief respite," said de Quincy, "and then either the king or the pope himself will shred the entire agreement! And we'll be left with nothing."

"You will not be left with nothing!" Langton replied sharply. "Fellow Christian men, we are facing a journey across a wild and unpredictable sea. We may not reach our final port of liberty in the same boat with which we embark. But we will get there! And we need this vessel, this covenant, this great charter to be where we begin our voyage! And if it is mocked, or disregarded, or nullified, always return to it. May it be as what Joshua said of old about the promises of Almighty God, that not one of them have fallen to the ground!"

The arrival of King John's forces and many servants could be heard from a great distance, even with the sodden ground absorbing the impact of feet and hoofs. The barons stood at the ready on one end of the meadow, while the king's forces arrayed opposite them. A simple dais, erected quickly with a portable throne, stood in the center of the glade, and here sat King John with an expectant look.

Taking the sheepskin parchment from William, Langton turned and marched toward the dais and bowed to the king, who returned his gesture with a haughty smirk and outstretched arms. A wren, its brown wings fluttering through the air, bisected the path between archbishop and king and uttered a sweet series of chirps.

"Archbishop Langton, my trusted negotiator," the king bellowed. "You have truly demonstrated to these barons there is no need for further hostilities. I trust you have in your hand the documents for my assent?"

Langton straightened himself. What I am about to share with him, he thought, has never been done to any king in the history of mankind. Almighty God, give me strength.

"O King," he began, "these barons have come to give you homage..."

"We already knew that, Your Grace!" John replied.

"Begging your pardon, Your Majesty," Langton interrupted, "but I was not finished."

John scowled at Langton, but at the same time shrank back in his chair. "Go on."

"The barons," Langton continued, "have come to give you homage. But it is the homage of a new day, of a new kingdom. Your agents have been with me and have given their word that you will give this great charter full attention. And as you do so, you will see that your power will never again be so rampant and intemperate."

"Then you were not there with my family at chapel yesterday for Trinity Sunday, dear Langton," chortled the king. "The fourth chapter of the Revelation of St. John.

Excellent name, if I may say so, and an excellent vision. Twenty-four elders bowing before the Divine King who was the color of jasper and carnelian." John wiggled his fingers to the archbishop, flashing his jeweled rings. "And they cast their crowns before the throne, and said "Worthy are you to receive glory and honor and power."' He flashed a brilliant smile to Langton. "Do you not sense this from those barons today, Langton? Bowing before me and throwing away their crowns?"

Langton stood firm. "You see that as a metaphor for what is to come this day?"

King John sighed, a sound of satisfaction, but his smile quickly disappeared.

Langton took two steps toward the throne and held out the parchment. "How do you not know it might be your crown, O King, that is cast along the floor?"

John took the sheepskin from Langton and, with the help of two servant pages, unrolled the charter and began to read. For five minutes, the king perused the scripted document. Langton noticed his face flush red from the first words, then erupt with rage at the end of the sheepskin. Looking up and glaring directly into Langton's eyes, the king roared.

"What in the name of heaven is this?" The king pointed to the initial words. "To say We have granted to God and confirmed by this charter, that the English Church shall be free?" He scoured the script again. "Free elections for your Church? Are you trying to anger me or Pope Innocent more?"

"I am more concerned not to anger our Lord Christ," Langton spoke plainly. "I know you believe you hold sway over priests, bishops, and churches in our land. I know the pope believes he holds sway over the same. I know each of you believes the other is wrong. I simply am saying you both are. The English Church is free from both you and Rome. And I am willing to stake my life on it."

King John's lips curled into an ugly sneer. "And you really think that will cause this charter to last?" he pouted. "The council of barons—the one mentioned toward the very end—you believe has the strength, the right to restrict me?" He stood and barked across the meadow at the assembled barons. "I am John, first of that name, and King of England, possessor of that title by divine right and blessing!" He turned to Langton in full fury. "This charter will not see the light of day past the end of this month. I shall annul it even after I agree to it. The pope shall do the same and turn on you! What do you have to say for yourself, Langton, you traitor?"

Stephen Langton set his jaw, absorbing every wave of the king's rage. Out of the corner of his eye, he saw Richard de Clare move toward them. Without looking, the archbishop held out his left hand and commanded the baron to remain where he was.

"Your Majesty," he answered the king, "two replies. The first is that although you are king, you serve at God's pleasure, not your own. Christ alone is the King of all that is, and He raises up and brings low the monarchs of this earth."

Leering at the archbishop, King John growled. "And the second thing?"

Langton leaned forward and pointed at the sheepskin. "Agree, annul, shred, disregard...whatever you choose to do against this does not matter, Your Majesty. Spit on the barons and they will stay your power. Destroy this charter and it will rise in new form again. Tear it apart and it will endure, no matter how many revisions, no matter what force you array against it! These words shall triumph, for they are part of this great charter, which shall outlive Your Majesty!"

The king continued to glare at Langton, but even the archbishop could see it was a spiteful resignation.

"Scribes," John called to several men on the west end of the dais. "Take this, and Archbishop Langton with you. Make ready with sheepskin, quill pens, and ink of the oak gall, and make the copies for our possession." He paused, then stood, unsteadily at first, and looked over all assembled at the meadow.

"To this charter," King John bellowed, "I give my full agreement."

Both sides erupted in cheers and song. Langton bowed his head and covered his heart with his hands as he prayed. Thank you, Lord Jesus, for giving strength to me, to Your people, to Your Church, and for granting this birth of liberty.

STEPHEN LANGTON served as the Archbishop of Canterbury from 1207 until his death in 1228. Overseeing spiritual and state affairs during a tumultuous era in England, Langton was also known for his passion for Scripture, and he divided the books of the Bible into the standard modern arrangement of chapters that we use today. This showdown at Runnymede between the barons and King John brought about the agreement known as Magna Carta, the Great Charter of Liberties, which protected the rights of free men in England. Although the original version was nullified soon after by both King John and Pope Innocent III, Langton never budged from his principles. Magna Carta was eventually confirmed as English law, the first time in post-biblical history that restraints on kings were specified in writing, and it greatly influenced other charters such as the American Declaration of Independence.

FRANCIS OF ASSISI

September 1219, Damietta, Egypt

The bright sun beat down upon the two travelers as the afternoon breezes wafted in from the Mediterranean Sea, blunting the stifling heat. Both the stocky older man and his younger, leaner friend shuffled along the path toward the city walls, marking well to remain several yards behind their mounted escorts and well ahead of the rear guard. Pulling a damp scarf to his face to avoid the swirling sand, the younger spoke for the first time.

"A few moments more and we shall be at the city gates, Brother Carlo," he said expectantly.

"I know your excitement, Friar Francis," Carlo replied, "although I am unsure what good will come of it. Still, it is good to get out of the camp even to enter the underbelly of the enemy."

"That is what a cease-fire is for, my good brother in Christ," Francis spoke, sweeping his eyes over the contours of the city walls, pockmarked with smashed stone and charred wood lining on the ramparts. The Crusaders had certainly done extensive damage but had been unable to breach the thick fortifications from land. The Frisian[1] navy had overrun the local port and held a strong blockade from the sea but had not been successful at taking Damietta itself. The effort on each side had exhausted Crusaders and Turks both, and at the end of the last month, a cease-fire was given full accord. Now, Francis thought, perhaps

1. The Frisians were medieval Germanic people who lived on the coast of what is now the Netherlands.

I have the opportunity to provide for God's creatures through the Gospel what the sword could not win. But he had no time to muse for now. They were nearly at the gates, and the Ayyubid[2] commander turned to them, mounted on his steed, his hand on the hilt of his sword.

"Christians, here I bear you forth into the city. Friar Francis, you shall have three hours to meet and speak with the Sultan. I do not have to impress upon you that it is important you allow him to speak first. No man addresses the Sultan until spoken to. Is that clear?"

"Commander," Francis bowed his head slightly, "it is most clear. May peace be upon you."

The commander backed up his horse and gave the command for the city gates to be opened. As Francis and Carlo walked by, he raised his hand in respect and replied, "Wa alaikum salaam."

There was no doubt as to the residence of Sultan Al-Kamil. The spacious palace was straight ahead, and Francis doubled his pace as Carlo pleaded with him to slow down.

"Are you the one they call the preacher?" bawled the Sultan from his chair, his barrel chest thrust in front of him. "Come forth, for it has been told me that you make entreaty during this calm but dark hour!"

Francis nodded to Carlo, who stood to the side, and he began to approach Al-Kamil. The Sultan looked intently at him, his bronze brow furrowing with questions. His trimmed beard was dark and slick with scented lotions, and Francis saw him dipping bread into a bowl of onions and spiced oil before taking a generous bite. Francis came within twelve feet of the ruler and halted, bowing slowly.

"Rise, man of noble, if misguided, faith," commanded the Sultan. "Your posture shows no fear; your face shows

2. The dynasty of Egypt's rulers when the Muslims re-took much of that land from the Crusaders under the general Saladin.

no discord. I believe I should receive you as a friend, and I would like to hear what you have come to say."

"What I have to say may surprise you, O Sultan," Francis replied. "I have come to your court to bring a message of hope that can set you free from the discord that surrounds this city."

"If you speak of negotiations," Al-Kamil grunted, "I would urge you to save your breath. Our warriors will defend this city to the last stone, as your Crusaders defended Jerusalem many years ago. Damietta might not have the glory of Cairo or Alexandria, but it is the home of my family and people and I will not yield to a suggestion that we surrender."

"I come offering you safety today," Francis humbly replied, stroking his head and the thinning wisps of hair atop it, "but not in the manner you assume. This message has nothing to do with swords and spears. Yes, there is a great struggle afoot, O Sultan, but it is one in which the battlefield is your heart."

Al-Kamil frowned, and leaned forward saying, "How do you mean, the battlefield is my heart? And who are you to make such a declaration?"

"You mean this humble and poor man who stands before you?" Francis asked.

"Yes, the one dragging in more dust and sand than we have seen in a fortnight!" cackled a well-dressed official standing to the right of the Sultan.

"Peace, Ashraf," Al-Kamil snapped. "The Christian may be a misguided messenger, but you will afford him the respect I give him!" He turned to Francis. "Your plain appearance does intrigue me...how should I address you?"

"Friar Francis."

"Friar Francis, very well. To what do I owe this blandness of dress that nonetheless exudes confidence of stature?"

"To do so requires that I tell you a bit of my story, O Sultan."

Al-Kamil's face broke into a toothy smile as he leaned back in his chair. "All the better, Friar Francis. I love a good tale."

Francis nodded toward the ruler and began. "I spent my tender years in Assisi, the place of my birth, a few days' journey from Rome. My father was a skillful and highly-respected silk merchant who expected his son would follow him into the family business. I lived the life of a son of wealth and enjoyed it greatly. As a result, the lavish decorations and plush interior of this court, not to mention your ornate clothing, O Sultan, do not seem strange, for they bring memories from my youth. I had devoted friends, loved to play as a troubadour and storyteller, and was dressed in the finest clothes. Yet, for all the wealth we possessed, it could not overlay the nagging emptiness in my heart. Then one day when I was selling cloth, silk, and velvet to folk in the local market a beggar happened to draw near. He was well known in the village. He asked me if I could spare him any food or clothing. And when he asked that, the light of heaven came ablaze in his eyes. I became aware chiefly of two things: his hope that he could be content, and my own utter worthless pursuit of joy through wealth."

The Sultan cocked his head to one side, amazed that anyone would confess to such stirrings of the heart in his presence. "Go on," he said, thinking that if these were military negotiations, they were the strangest ones he'd ever experienced!

"The hope that shone on his face stayed with me," Francis continued, "and so by the time the day was over and I had sold all my wares I began to ponder something the priest had said during Mass the previous Sunday, about how St. Peter said the disciples had left everything to follow Jesus. I realized if I truly wished to follow Christ, then I must be willing to do the same. I ran after the beggar, gave him all the money I accumulated from that day's sales, and returned home. Needless to say, my father was not amused."

"Nor would I be, as a father," Al-Kamil replied grudgingly.

"My friends mocked me; my father exploded with rage. Even then, my desire for Christ did not take root as it should. For a time I served as a soldier, and, while I fell ill during my time as a prisoner of war, I began to think why I felt at such peace when I had given the money to the beggar. I came to see that it was the spirit of Christ dwelling within me prodding me toward such action. This I believed needed to control my entire life. I went home upon my release and told my father I was renouncing the world and its wealthy trappings and giving myself fully to proclaiming the teachings of Jesus. I would live simply, in poverty, accepting sustenance from others as gifts from His hand."

"You have lived this way from then on?" Al-Kamil spoke, stunned.

"I stripped my clothes and went to the bishop, exclaiming that I was willing to go without for the sake of Christ. My father thought I was insane; my former friends still believe so. But my hardy band of fellow friars[3]—that is the name for our band of traveling preachers—and I continue on, living in community, serving the poor, teaching others, offering ourselves to Christ."

The Sultan eased back in his padded chair, brushing aside a servant to his left who was fanning him with a large palm leaf. "Your passion for goodness is noble, Friar Francis. I am not doubting your intentions. Yet, I must admit to being confused, for I thought that your approach during this cease-fire was to offer negotiations. While I have heard your story, which is interesting, I don't know what your true intent might be."

3. Friar: a member of a certain religious order of men, especially the four mendicant orders (Augustinians, Carmelites, Dominicans, and Franciscans).

"What else would it be other than to offer the hope of life in Jesus Christ before you, O Sultan?"

"Christ?" Al-Kamil scoffed harshly, his respect for Francis clashing with his disdain for the message he sensed the poor friar bore to his court. "I hope you recognize I have nothing against the man you call Jesus. Even within our great noble faith of Islam, we hold this Jesus in the highest regard. He is one of the prophets of Allah, a moral teacher of the highest nature. He is not Allah, nor even Muhammad the prophet, peace be upon him. But even though I do not share your same passion for this Jesus, you should certainly see I have no stake against Him!"

"None, truly?" asked Francis plainly.

"Something tells me you are not convinced."

"Jesus Himself a prophet, a great moral teacher of the highest nature, I believe you said?"

"You were standing here, Francis," the Sultan replied evenly. "Certainly, you heard my words clearly."

"Then we clearly have a clash of visions, O Sultan," said Francis. "The Jesus who received worship and prayer, who forgave the sins of others, who could see into the hearts of those who spoke both for and against Him...these are all things that can only be done by God Himself! Was Jesus God who became man so that we could be sons of God? Or was He lying? Or deluded? Did He know who He was?"

"He was a prophet of Allah, Francis," Al-Kamil retorted more strongly than he wished. "Nothing beyond that."

"Then how could a prophet of Allah be so mistaken about Himself? Why would He receive worship or forgive sins then?"

"He might have misspoke about who He was," offered the Sultan.

"Why would a prophet misspeak?"

"He could have been ignorant."

"A prophet of God? Truly?"

"Friar Francis, you are angering me beyond what is reasonable! And it is obvious you have not read a word of the Qur'an!"

"You might be surprised, O Sultan," Francis replied. "But there is another question I have for you. Do you believe that when your last breath escapes your body, you will stand before Allah the merciful?"

"I certainly hope my life's deeds will show a balance that will gain me entry to heaven."

"Then Allah is not merciful."

"How dare you!"

"Answer the charge, my good Sultan," Francis said unflinchingly. "For if your way is true, what do you have to fear? If your salvation depends on the weight of your life's work, then Allah neither extends mercy nor needs to display it. Do not your teachers proclaim that the one who wanders bears the entire burden of returning to the hands of Allah?"

"Most certainly," Al-Kamil muttered, his voice having grown considerably softer now, "I was wrong to underestimate a poor friar like yourself."

"Then allow me to invite you to consider one more thing. If you wander, do you wish to wander from a Judge who sternly demands your return and offers no mercy? Or do you wish for a brother, a friend who will pursue you as far as you go from Him?"

"I admit this was not what I was expecting."

Francis straightened up to his full height. "I am not here to negotiate a settlement between the armies of Europe and the Ayyubids. That is beyond my power. And if you are truly honest, even as you are the son of the brother of the great Saladin, it is beyond your skill and cunning."

Al-Kamil suddenly rose from his chair, taking a few deliberate, unthreatening steps toward Francis and placed his hands firmly on his shoulders, staring into the friar's eyes. "Then what are you here for?"

"O Sultan, I am here to negotiate that you consider whose kingdom you follow. Is it the one that Allah offers? Or the one that Christ alone rules and offers with grace and joy to the subjects for whom He bled and died?" He waved off Al-Kamil's objections. "No, I am well aware of what the Qur'an would say. Nonetheless, know that I am not seeking an end to this war outside the city. I am seeking you to come to peace in the war for your heart. And I would beg you to consider the consequences."

Al-Kamil thought for several moments before nodding to his guards at the door. "The time is up, Friar Francis, and you must return to the camp. I cannot thank you for the substance of what you said, but I respect you and am grateful for the way you said it. The chasm between us is fixed too far to join our faiths, but you have come with concern and mourning for my spirit. And if nothing else, I am grateful for your kindness."

"I thank you, O Sultan, with the reminder I will never stop praying for you, and I hope that the Jesus who captured me will capture you, as well."

"Even if this is the last we ever see of each other?" the Sultan replied.

Francis nodded and smiled kindly before turning toward the door. "The Lord has seen to my every need and care. He cares for the animals and birds to whom I sing every day with joy. And He can watch over you. And I will always pray He does."

FRANCIS OF ASSISI left behind a comfortable life at a young age, and in 1210 he founded the Order of Friars Minor (known more popularly as the Franciscans), a movement based on simplicity, poverty, charity, and obedience to the radical call of Christ. This story also depicts another of his passions: preaching Christ. In 1219 during the Fifth Crusade, Francis crossed enemy lines during a cease-fire, attempting to convince the Sultan for the Gospel. One of the most beloved individuals in Christian history, he achieved a legacy of imitating Christ and showing respect for all human beings and all creatures. He even preached to the birds and called animals his "brothers and sisters", showing a profound love for nature as the fingerprints of God (the hymn "All Creatures of Our God and King" is based on a paraphrase of a poem by Francis). His sweetness of character and his concern for the poor are remembered highly to the present day.

UKRAINE
AUSTRIA
MOLDOVA
ROMANIA
CROATIA
SERBIA
BULGARIA
ITALY
GREECE
TURKEY
SYRIA
LEBANON
ISRAEL
JORDAN
LIBYA
EGYPT

DAMETTA

THOMAS AQUINAS

1248, Cologne, Holy Roman Empire

Bursting through the door, the young man gathered his cassock[1] and quickly walked down the south cloister, without even a backwards glance. The sneering comments and brutal barbs that had been thrown at him were proving too much to bear. Clenching his jaw tightly shut, he blinked back tears. I will not cry, he told himself, recognizing the lie as soon as his mind expressed it. That is, I will not cry until I can find a place to hide.

After a minute he turned down a side path leading toward the school. He found his way back to his room just as the first drops of what threatened to be a savage rainstorm began to lash at his tonsured head. Pulling the latch on his door, the student practically leaped into the sanctuary of his abode, slamming the door shut and taking a chair to lodge beneath the latch from inside. Stupid rule against locks, stupid willingness to trust others, he grumbled to himself. But the anger gave way to self-pity in an instant, and yielding to the grief of the moment, the young man thrust himself upon his austere bed and began to weep.

Why, O why do they treat me this way? He thought. Did God foresee this when I followed the master here? Why didn't I accept the leadership of Monte Cassino? I would never have had to put up with this abuse!

"Idiot!"

"Mumbler!"

---

1. A clerical coat or ankle length garment.

"Stupid sheep!"

"Get the words out, you dumb ox!"

The insults came back to mind as if a dam had burst in his heart. The man breathed, in and out, more slowly, desperately trying to calm his anguished spirit. Only a few moments had gone by that seemed like hours when he heard a gentle knock on his door.

"Go away!" he choked. "I am indisposed!"

A pause, then the same knock, the same cadence, gentler this time.

"Did you not hear me?" he screamed at the wooden frame.

The latch wiggled, and then a kind voice came from the other side of the door. "I did hear, you, Thomas, but I still think it would be more useful if I could speak to you in your room rather than from the opposite side of this plank of wood."

Thomas silently rebuked himself for his outburst. To be that disrespectful toward Master Albertus, he angrily mused. How shameful. He didn't deserve that! Stumbling across the floor, Thomas moved the chair and opened the door.

"Master," he sniffed. "Please enter."

Albertus Magnus nodded and entered the sparse quarters, easing into the cramped area and looking patiently for a place to sit. Thomas shut the door as he pondered about the journey that led him here. Assigned to teach at the Studium Generale here in Cologne, Albertus had convinced Thomas to spurn Pope Innocent IV's offer to oversee Benedict's former monastery of Monte Cassino. Instead, he followed him eastward from Paris, where Thomas had previously studied under Albertus. In the end, the offer of being named Albertus' master student was too enticing. Now, reflecting on his performance this first term, and how he would freeze in class at the slightest attempt to give worthy answers, Thomas would not blame Albertus if this was a meeting to say this journey was now at an end.

Albertus saw a wooden chair and seated himself, looking around the room. A simple bed cover was spread over Thomas' mattress. A table was piled with books and papers. Thomas' clothes were folded neatly on a bench against the far wall. Albertus smiled.

"You've made good use of your space here, Thomas," he chuckled. "Your clothing is neatly tucked away, and your life of the mind is stacked properly. Exactly as a scholar's should be."

"I am a scholar," Thomas scoffed, staring at the floor and not even raising his eyes, "Every time you ask a question and the offer to answer comes to me, I can do nothing. I choke up. I stutter and stammer. All this would be bad enough as it is, but these failures are those of your 'master scholar'. Dear teacher," he said dejectedly, "that is a weight that I cannot carry."

Thomas had thrown the words through the air at Albertus as one would throw a knife at a target. He fully expected a vile rebuke from his teacher, but what followed was anything but.

"Thomas," he replied, "do you recall my advice in Paris when you faced a difficult dilemma on Aristotle's view of the ideal choice between two extremes?"

It was Thomas' turn to emit a dry chuckle. "I believe that was my first year under your teaching, sir," he responded. "And you said, 'In a difficult test, divide the question.'"

"Then let us do that here," Albertus stood up suddenly, his posture straight, his commanding form hovering over Thomas. "But instead let us divide the statement that you just presented to me." He rubbed his face and turned around as a rumble of thunder announced the further dance of rain upon the grass outside.

"Thomas, you said you can do nothing ?"

"Exactly."

"You choke up?"

"Yes."

"You stutter and stammer?"

"Yes, teacher. All these things are exactly as I told you. I am an abject failure here."

"Ah-ah," Albertus stopped him quickly. "Divide the matter. Those are events that happened. Those are actions you did, or didn't do, as the case may be. I do not say that is who you are!"

"And yet it is exactly why the other students mock and spite me!" Thomas cried. "Stupid mumbler? Empty-headed fool? Dumb ox? Select what you will, master. There are plenty of insults they give me!" "Insults do not make the man, Thomas! Your reactions to such denigrations will shape who you are," Albertus cautioned. "Do you really think I would view you as my master student if you were not gifted accordingly?"

"Right now, master," Thomas replied wearily, "you could take all I know about myself, set it on this table, place a feather upon it, and watch the feather crush that amount beneath it."

Albertus leaned back in the chair, unleashing a hearty laugh that shook the room. "I am glad you have kept your sense of humor, my son," he cackled, "but I want you to bring your keen mind and wise heart to our gathering tomorrow, because you will open the minds of others to what is in there."

"And bring on even more of their insults in the lecture hall?" asked Thomas.

"Forget the lecture hall," Albertus answered. "It is not your mind that is confused; it is the setting that is so confusing. But I don't want to give away my secret. Just trust me. Class time tomorrow. Meet me there with the others, and then I believe you will amaze even your greatest skeptics."

"Where are we going?" blurted out Otto, one of the other students. "Master, why are we headed outside when the grass is sure to be slick from yesterday's downpour?"

"If God created the natural world around us, Otto," remarked Albertus Magnus, "then it's assuredly good for us to enjoy it, whether wet or dry." The cluster of fourteen students moved with Albertus onto the grassy ridge outside the academy's walls, Thomas anxiously bringing up the rear. As Albertus slowed to a halt, the students formed a semicircle around him.

"Now, there is a reason I've asked you to leave your books back in the lecture hall," the teacher began. "I know that you could always reference your answers to any of my questions by pointing to the text by which you prove your responses. That has its place, but not so today. This day, I wish you to use what you see around you to support your claims."

"In this glade, master?" asked another student with a trace of mockery in his tone. "Under the sun amongst the flowers?"

"Yes, let's see how we might apply our learning outdoors." Albertus folded his arms and looked hard at the array of students before him. "We have been speaking of our rational nature, as Aristotle spoke of many years ago. As a reminder, how did Aristotle describe man?"

A burly classmate shot a glance at Thomas, then looked at Albertus and raised his own hand. "Aristotle called man 'the rational animal.'"

"Does that seem too brutal to you?" asked Albertus.

"He has to think that," joked Otto, "since he's more animal than rational man."

"Funny how you're saying that from twenty feet away and not next to me," growled the stocky student.

"Calm yourselves, men," Albertus smiled, warily keeping an eye on Thomas. "Well, how might we answer?"

"Isn't it accurate, master?" the large one replied, shrugging his broad shoulders. "We are rational beings, and our goal is the use of pure reason to discern our world."

"All of it?" came the sound of a detached, dreamy voice. All heads turned in its direction, shocked. It came from Thomas, who wasn't looking at the others, his attention distracted by a patch of cornflowers growing in the soil near the base of the hill.

"What do you mean, all of it?" Otto asked before being surprised that Thomas had ignored their company and began walking down the hill to the flowerbed.

Albertus waved the group onward. Otto piped up, "Come on, men. Let's see what the dumb ox will forget by the time he gets there."

The whole class, Albertus included, clambered down the hill to where Thomas was already stooped low and gazing intently at one of the cornflowers. Touching the blue, finger-like petals, he stared closely, as if he could divine from the delicate flower itself some deep truth that would fulfill the question Albertus had posed.

"Why, the dumb-ox is trying to find his reflection in a flower," a wise-cracking student sniggered. But Thomas ignored him and then blurted out suddenly, "It is not!"

"It is not what?" asked Albertus in reply.

Thomas stood and looked at his teacher and fellow pupils. "It is not accurate!" He looked at his master. "Aristotle spoke truth that we are rational, we are beasts endued with reason. But that cannot be all that we are!"

"What are you saying, Thomas?" another person inquired.

Thomas knelt down again, twisting his body so that he could look back at their group as he gestured around the cornflower. "It struck me just as I saw this flower," he said breathlessly from excitement. “We are human beings, granted reason to see the world and ascertain what it is. And that is a helpful thing. That is the nature granted us. But that is not all we are!” He pointed at the center of the flower, and then let his fingers dance around the intricate parts. “To say that is all we are would be like saying this cornflower is complete with only the stigma, the stamens, and the filament at the center. Can we imagine finding joy in that? I myself would find it difficult!” He looked around at his fellow classmates – no one was mocking him now. “Almighty God has created us to be more than that! He has created us to reflect His nature, and not just as ‘rational animals’! Yes, we have reason and mindfulness as this flower has its central component parts. But we also are dressed with the beauty of God’s image as the petals surround this flower! So yes, Aristotle speaks truthfully, but he does not go far enough! God dresses us in His grace and His glory as this flower is dressed with the strikingly beautiful blue petals that surround its center!”

“This is fascinating, Thomas!” Albertus exclaimed, with several of the pupils nodding in agreement. “I just have one question to follow, though. While a flower can remain beautiful and unspoiled, our being is affected by sin against God, isn’t it?”

Thomas took in a quick gulp of air, momentarily panicking. What? He looked down at the cornflower. That won’t do for my answer! His mind raced and his eyes scanned the field. “Ah!” he called out, pointing ahead to a rotting tree standing fifty yards away. “Look to that! Look to the tree!”

“It’s rotten and decaying, Thomas,” replied Otto. “What’s your contention?”

“And why is it rotten and decaying, Otto?” Thomas said, his voice bursting with frenzy and passion. “What do you think?”

"Not to take Otto's right to answer," said another, "but my father is an arborist in Arnsberg and he would say it could be several things. Perhaps the tree is infected with disease. Or it could be the location."

"Meaning what?" Thomas implored the students, waggling his hands around in a circular fashion, the frenzy of discovery driving him on.

"It could be the soil," the burly student answered. "Our family had the same situation occur on our estate in Saint-Denis. We had a young oak that sprouted but the limbs would fray and we could never get it to grow. Then we noticed patches of dry ground exposed around it. We dug up the oak and planted it in another part of the field, where it grew to full height." He smiled. "It happens to be my favorite place to rest outside when I am home."

"And that is the point," Thomas grinned. "We have our rational nature. We are given God's image. As we are planted in the sin that Adam brought into our world, we need rescued from our nature and given grace." He stood up, inhaled, and exhaled deeply, joy flooding his soul. "God plants us in His grace, and we grow healthy, strong, and able to serve Him!"

He paused, and in that moment every man around him began, slowly at first and then with faster cadence, to clap enthusiastically. Soon the entire area around the flowerbed thundered with applause as the previously scornful students raised Thomas up on their shoulders, carrying him up the hill back to the academy with joyful shouts.

Albertus watched the crowd inch up the hill, flabbergasted by what they had just seen. Finally, Otto, who had stayed behind, turned to Albertus.

"Is this why you brought us out here, sir? Was it for Thomas as much as for us?"

"The lecture hall is our creation. The natural world is God's creation," Albertus admitted. "Perhaps Thomas would be more confident speaking of the things of God using the elements that God placed before us." He smiled broadly. "I'm happy to see it worked."

Otto shook his head in admiration and amazement. "He's no longer the dumb ox that we thought he was."

"Whether others continue to call him that is yet to be seen," Albertus replied, "but I believe this about Thomas: One day, that ox will certainly fill the world with his bellowing!"

THOMAS AQUINAS became one of the great thinkers and writers of the medieval church. Born in Aquino, Italy in 1225, he pursued a life with the "preaching monks" of the Dominican order. Studying at Naples and Paris, he eventually followed his revered teacher Albertus Magnus to Cologne (now in Germany). Struggling to overcome his stammering and slowness of speech, eventually others recognized his brilliance and his passion for Scripture and philosophy. His greatest literary work, a conversational volume called the *Summa Theologica,* was the greatest theological work of the Middle Ages, integrating the best of Greek philosophy with Christian teaching. One of Thomas' greatest contributions to philosophy is his series of five arguments, or proofs, for the existence of God, while he always remained humble to say we can know God clearly, but never fully.

FACT FILES

Mystics, Great Leaders, Strange Movements, and Divisions

The Middle Ages brought the rise of a complex collection of individuals and groups. Some spoke forth to unite Christendom, while others were more responsible for fractures within the Church. All of them, however, were people of unyielding desire and passion.

Catherine of Siena and Thomas à Kempis were two of the major mystics of this period. Mysticism arose partly as a reaction to the scholarly nature of Catholic theology. Mystics undertook practices and uttered prayers designed to bring the human soul into more direct contact with God and enjoy the unfettered presence of Christ through the Holy Spirit. Catherine left her home in Siena, Italy, in the 1360s to enter the Dominican order of nuns in Florence. She beheld a series of powerful visions in which she received a vivid awareness of the love and presence of Christ. Eager for the peace of the Church at a time of great division, Catherine prayed and confessed before God at the expense of her physical health. Thomas à Kempis was a German mystic who spent time ministering in the Netherlands at the Mount Saint Agnes monastery, which he entered in 1399. His most magnificent work is *The Imitation of Christ*, a simple, direct book aimed at guiding its readers into a more intentional journey of living as Christians. Thomas' two desires were that his readers should purposefully embrace heavenly goals and divine hope every day, walking with Jesus while engaging in the everyday activity of human life. Thomas' practical, devotional effort has proved popular with Christians of all traditions over the years, and it has been read and translated into more languages than any other book besides the Bible.

Aside from the mystics, other personalities brought their considerable gifts to the realm of theology, particularly the sacraments. It was Paschasius Radbertus who explored the matter of the Lord's Supper, or the Eucharist, with notable interest. Radbertus endured a famous dispute with fellow French monk Ratramnus over the nature of the bread and wine in the Communion meal. In 831, Radbertus argued that when the bread and wine of Communion are consecrated (set apart by the priest as items for holy use) they change into the body and blood of Jesus Christ. The bread and wine will seem like actual food and drink, but they have been changed. His contemporary Ratramnus argued against this, saying the bread and wine remained physical food and drink while spiritually acting as Christ's body and blood for the believer. Radbertus, however, was careful to note that believers ate and drank Jesus' being in a spiritual sense. Even Radbertus believed Jesus' ascended, historical body was in heaven. In time, more Church leaders grew to embrace Radbertus' view, which developed even further into what became known as transubstantiation.

Although much of our story has focused on western Europe, the East was a location for dynamic leaders to arise on behalf of Christianity. Although Christianity made an initial entrance into Russia when Olga, Princess of Kiev, was baptized in 957, it was Olga's grandson Vladimir who fully Christianized his nation. It is said that Vladimir—wanting to make an informed decision of which faith to follow—invited representatives from the Catholic Church in the West, the Orthodox Church in the Byzantine Empire of Constantinople, Judaism, and Islam. While Vladimir firmly decided against Judaism and Islam, he wanted to explore each branch of Christianity further and so sent representatives to both Rome and Constantinople. The delegation that went to experience Orthodoxy came away from the worship and splendor of Hagia Sophia Cathedral profoundly awed. Opting for the beauty of Orthodox worship, Vladimir and his court members received baptism in the Dnieper River in 988. Vladimir then promoted the development of worship and theology in the Russian language, and he also fashioned a system of help and assistance for the poor and needy in his kingdom.

Back in the West, a Franciscan monk and thinker named John Bonaventure (1221-1274) led the Catholic Church on a path that combined the best of the scholarly pursuits of Anselm, the philosophical ability of Thomas Aquinas, and the mysticism that would emerge with Catherine of Siena and Thomas à Kempis. A firm believer that faith must initiate any pursuit of true knowledge, Bonaventure wrote *The Journey of the Mind Into God,* considered his greatest work. In it, he demonstrates that trust in Christ leads to understanding and reason that builds faith on a path of prayer, and delight that unites one's soul memorably to God. In addition, Bonaventure was insistent that people are unable to be made right with God unless given the gift of grace that justifies them. Only then can one be changed more into the image of Christ. Another great writer was the Florence poet Dante Alighieri (1265-1321), whose magnificent work The Divine Comedy became far and away the finest poem of the Middle Ages. The Divine Comedy was essential for several reasons. First, it gave bold, imaginative color to the Church's doctrine of life after death in three separate works, taking the reader on an extended, rhythmic journey through the many layers each of hell (Inferno) on through purgatory (Purgatorio)—which Catholics believe in and Protestant Christians do not—and heaven (Paradisio). Dante also broke new ground by writing his grand poetry in Italian rather than Latin, making it accessible to more ordinary literate people beyond just the educated elite.

Not all theologians speculated and thought well. In the Middle Ages, there were a number of heretical movements that denied fundamental truths of the Christian faith, yet nonetheless these groups claimed to be the true Church. In what is now Bulgaria, the Bogomils came to prominence in the tenth century, named after a priest named Bogomils who revived teachings of ancient Gnosticism. Denying the Old Testament, the Bogomils taught the physical world was evil and controlled by Satan, that marriage and meat-eating were forbidden, and they used no physical items in their worship (so, no baptism or Communion). They also taught that Satan was Christ's younger brother and that Christ came to earth to teach a better way. He died but rose again in a spirit form. They believed that Salvation comes to people who desire to be set free of their evil physical bodies by the influence of Jesus. Although the Bogomils flourished for some time and sent missionaries to western Europe, the heresy died out when the Muslims conquered their territory in the late fourteenth century. Their influence lived on in the Cathars of Albi, France, who held to many of the Bogomils' teachings. Proclaiming that the devil Satan was just as powerful as God, the Cathars went further than the Bogomils, teaching that Jesus had no physical body, never died, and never rose from the dead. Spiritual awakening, not Christ's work on the Cross, saves us, claimed the Cathars. In addition, marriage and reproduction were forbidden. But what truly earned them the hatred of the Catholic Church was the Cathars' insistence they were the true church of Christ on earth and alone could be saved. Going even further, they declared the Pope was the Antichrist on earth, which brought on the wrath of Rome itself. Pope Innocent III, no stranger to military offensives, proclaimed a war in 1209—known as the Albigensian Crusade—to crush the Cathars mercilessly in a slaughter of men, women, and children. While the Cathars' beliefs were not biblical, they hardly earned the savagery of the Catholic response.

Along with the challenges of heretics, the Christian movement found itself riven in two over a number of years in a divide that eventually fractured the West (Catholic Church) from the East (Orthodox Church). Since the Council of Chalcedon in 451, the two groups had gradually grown apart well in advance of the final break. Both churches faced their circumstances differently. Catholic worship was primarily conducted in Latin, while Orthodox communication was almost entirely in Greek, leading to difficulties when working through disagreements. Both churches also exhibited different emphases in their theology. The Catholic West focused on the question, "How do we become right with God?", and made much of Jesus' crucifixion while also rejoicing in the resurrection. The Orthodox East pursued the question, "How do we become God-like in union with Him?", and so the resurrection of Christ pointed the way to this goal while still giving thanks for Christ's death on the cross. Other clashes surfaced in ministry, the sacraments, and theology. Catholics required that no priests could marry; the Orthodox Church insisted bishops remain single, but priests could marry and have families. The Catholics used unleavened bread in the Eucharist, as opposed to the Orthodox bread containing yeast.

Fundamental differences on how the church made decisions also caused division. The West insisted that the Pope was the ultimate authority, while the East insisted on a more conciliary approach, where bishops, making decisions together ruled the church.

The Orthodox patriarch of Constantinople, Michael Cerularius, refused to admit that Pope Leo IX had authority over him, and on 16 July 1054, the pope's delegate, Cardinal Humbert walked into Hagia Sophia Cathedral in Constantinople, where Cerularius was celebrating the Eucharist. Slapping a declaration against the patriarch onto the altar, Humbert dusted off his feet and left the cathedral, signifying the definitive break between East and West.

JOHN WYCLIFFE

October 1380, Lutterworth, England

Slipping on the wet leaves leading into the cloister at St. Mary's Church, the preacher put forth the staff in his hand, bracing himself and preventing a sudden fall. The wind that swept down the cloister's path threatened to knock over the preacher, but he kept his footing and determination equally strong. I must not miss this evening above all, he reminded himself. Word had spread throughout the nation about his recent writings, and if they had spread all through England, he thought, certainly they were elsewhere. And if elsewhere, then he knew enemies lay in wait to confront him.

Thinking of the plan he had discussed with others a few hours ago, the preacher opened the side door of St. Mary's, entered the back hallway, and then felt for the latch on the door that led to the passageway into the pulpit.

The church's interior was already well-lit, casting a yellowish glow over the seated men in the front. The preacher ascended the pulpit and laid two sacks at his feet, drawing a massive book from one and placing it on the pulpit before him. Adjusting his wool cap, worn specifically so his head was not exposed to the Leicestershire chill, he smiled kindly and nodded to the men below.

"Good evening, my friends," he rasped.

"Good evening, Master Wycliffe," they murmured in reply.

John Wycliffe sighed, allowing the severity of the moment to sink in. These men, only a portion of his students and friends, allies in his ambitious resolve, held the success of this evening's events in their hands.

"I am obliged to mention," he began, "that the ears of England have been especially sharp these days. We should expect to be separated this evening and I could be questioned. I want you to be prepared to take up what I leave you for however long I might be detained."

"We will, Master Wycliffe," said one student in the front row. "But what instructions are you giving us in this moment?"

"I wish to make known the distribution of a work I recently published on the Eucharist," Wycliffe said wearily. "It is no surprise to any of you, given our recent discussions. But the book has gained a wide readership, and as such, we are facing a severe backlash from the Church even as we are covered by protection from the king and the people. Along with my previous statements about Holy Scripture and the Pope himself, I believe this book has made me the target of church authorities all over."

"Then what is it you wish us to do?" asked another earnest young man.

"What you do best," Wycliffe answered, a twinkle in his eye. "Take our written efforts and go out to teach the people. You can do this whether or not I am..."

"Silence!" cried a voice in the back of the church. Wycliffe looked up and his students turned around in sudden fear. A mail-clad guard, wearing the livery of the archbishop of Canterbury, held up one hand while holding a sword in his other, pointing the weapon directly at Wycliffe. "You, the one named Wycliffe. Bring that which is with you and come with me!" At those words, five more guards darted out of the shadows and stood, swords drawn. "Now! Hurry! And bring that accursed book with you!"

"No, Master," a diminutive young man squeaked in protest. But Wycliffe was already placing the book in the sack and descending the steps next to the pulpit.

"Have a care, men," he said gently, waving the soldiers forward to show he would come gladly. "If the Church wishes to discuss these matters with me I will go."

"And we have just the place," the guard replied gruffly.

"But, Master," a colleague whispered, drawing next to Wycliffe and lowering his voice so only the preacher could hear, "you said we would go out and teach the people! With what would we accomplish that?"

Wycliffe looked past him, giving an ever-so-imperceptible nod toward the pulpit. He replied with a secretive tone, "You will find your supplies at...your master's feet," before the guard roughly grabbed Wycliffe's arm.

"Now, Wycliffe," he ordered.

As Wycliffe departed, his friends and colleagues noticed his final glance towards the pulpit. There they found a second volume in a second hidden sack. Their mission was clear.

"More people for dinner hour?" bawled the red-faced publican from behind the serving table at the Swan Inn.[1]

"We are here for reasons of our own," roared the archbishop, slamming his fist on the table top as the guards approached from behind. "You will not stand against the Mother Church and deny us a place!"

"Oh, Master Wycliffe," said the publican's wife. "I didn't realize you were with this lot tonight!"

"This night, I am," Wycliffe said smoothly and kindly. "Could you make sure that enough ale is brought to our table and I will pay you for the full amount?"

"For you, Master Wycliffe, we obey," the publican nodded, taking several stoneware mugs and turning to the cask behind him.

Wycliffe likewise turned in the direction of the others within the pub. Guards and priests stared at him, surprised that he was not frightened out of his wits. The only one

1. A map of Medieval Lutterworth: https://www.le.ac.uk/lahs/downloads/2018/2018%20(92)%20P115-146%20Watkins.pdf

who wore no surprise was already seated, preening on his chair as if it was his throne at Lambeth Palace.

"Good evening, Master Wycliffe," growled the archbishop of Canterbury, Simon Sudbury. "Do be seated."

"Thank you, your Grace," Wycliffe replied, easing himself into a chair as twelve mugs of ale, one for each guest were deposited at the table.

Sudbury leaned across toward Wycliffe. "I do apologize for the sudden breach of decent manner, but I hope you realize that given your unorthodox state of communications lately, my actions are hardly out of order."

"That is for God and Holy Scripture to decide, your Grace," replied Wycliffe.

The archbishop slapped his hand on the table. "Seriously, Master Wycliffe, you sound like a madman repeating the same verbal squall without reason." He took a sip of his ale. "You showed up previously at Lambeth to defend yourself against heresy charges after repeated requests. You enjoy the good will of the king and the people in covering for you in time of need. So, we decided to come and deal with your latest round of trouble and bring you back to Canterbury by force after questioning you here."

"Thus, your decision is to come to Lutterworth," Wycliffe began. "And you think that your presence in a public inn will go unnoticed by the townspeople?"

"Keep your voice down, Wycliffe!" demanded Robert Stanford, the archbishop's chaplain.

"Quiet yourself, Robert," the archbishop said, staying the outburst with a wave of his hand. "In successive years, Wycliffe, you have declared yourself opposed to the doctrines of the Church, and we now move to come here so that your works might be taken and incinerated at Lambeth."

"Why?" Wycliffe asked, bemused, taking a long sip of his ale. "Are they contrary to Holy Scripture?"

The archbishop tried on a soothing air that possessed a trace of mockery. "We have been over this ground before. Your doctrines assault the Church, upon which the Scriptures are founded and out of which they receive their living character. You simply cannot raise such objections against the Church. And your mumbling Lollards will cease and desist from spreading your poisonous prattle!"

"By whose strength will you ensure that, Your Grace?" asked Wycliffe. "You think that men-at-arms will prevent the pure truth of God's Word from spreading."

"Your debate tricks are merely games," retorted Stanford. "You are playing with words!"

"Isn't that the essence of all speech?" Wycliffe inquired, before Sudbury thumped his empty mug down loudly on the table.

"Just so you are aware of why we are dislodging you from Lutterworth," he began, "let us review the facts before us. You have made trouble for the Church and breathe air into the rebellious spirit within this land that goes against the Church's leadership!"

"I seem to remember," said Wycliffe, that you uttered the exact same complaints when I published *The Truth of Holy Scripture.*"

"All of which proved you have turned the clear authority of the Church upside-down!" the archbishop sneered. "We are to test all things by the declarations of the holy Catholic Church, passed down from the early fathers, popes, and councils. You seem to have the novel idea that the followers of Christ must put the Church's teachings to the test under the authority of Scripture! What nonsense are you trying to bring into this world?"

"Can you please tell me then," Wycliffe replied, at great pains to disguise his rising temper, "how would the apostle Paul's charge to the Corinthians make any sense, therefore? When he plainly states, Examine yourselves to see if your faith is authentic...test yourselves!...Please tell me by which of your claimed authorities they would do so? Were there early church fathers beyond the apostles—who wrote the Scriptures—at that point? Were there any popes to pass judgment? Any great councils of note that they could use to examine their faith? What else would there have been but God's holy and living written Word?"

"You charlatan!" Sudbury nearly choked on his hatred. "The tragedy is not that you merely spoke such venom, but that you continued to spread it by challenging the very nature of the Church!"

"Ah, you have read my *On The Church,*" Wycliffe answered sarcastically. "I feared you had merely heard the rumors about it and lodged your own conclusions. You didn't care for how I defined the assembly of the faithful?"

"Giving no ground for the oversight of His Holiness and all the bishops and priests called to holy orders for the spiritual care of souls?" Sudbury's face flamed, his anger colliding with the alcohol coursing through his bloodstream. "Thomas Bradwardine dug his claws into you more than I gave him credit for."

"All he did was teach me Augustine," said Wycliffe, "and I followed the paths the Church neglected about itself."

"The Church of which the Pope is the head?"

"If by head, you mean the chief pastor of the visible churches clustered in Rome itself," Wycliffe replied evenly, "I have no issue with that. But that's where it ends. Look to the New Testament of our Lord Christ. At no point does the Bible define the Church as being under the control of popes and priests. Always we submit to Christ, a people who—as the true church—are chosen for and granted salvation by the undeserved, free grace of Almighty God. The Church is not the Pope's treasure chamber; it is the assembly of those treasured by Christ as His elect sheep."

"Scoundrel!" Stanford snapped. The Leicestershire ale was affecting his temper.

"Call me scoundrel if you wish, chaplain," Wycliffe grinned, "but if you take issue with what I say, you oppose Augustine himself. So much for fidelity to the early church fathers."

"Or for your fidelity to His Holiness," argued Sudbury. "For you have denied the papacy to have originated from Almighty God. You have claimed that any pope who does not follow Christ is the Antichrist."

"Savage beast," mumbled Stanford, wiping the ale suds from his chin. "You are despicable."

"Despicable indeed," the archbishop added, his voice quaking with rage. "You dare to say that the bread and wine of the Holy Eucharist remain as they are, that Christ's body and blood are nowhere to be found except spiritually? Do you not realize what a vile departure that is from the teachings of your Church?"

"Departing from false doctrine is what happens," Wycliffe replied, "when you provide access to the people to hear it read in their own language, which you seem determined to prevent!"

"And that is exactly what brings us to this point," Sudbury answered with a murderous look. "We know you have published your insane piece about the Eucharist. We know you have finished your copy of the New Testament in the English language. You will not hand over to the people any opportunity to corrupt what only bishops and priests are allowed to make plain!"

"What are you saying?" Wycliffe asked, looking out the window at a pack of several figures moving through the darkness, mounting horses and heading in all directions.

"Hand over your sack, John," his adversary ordered. "The fencing between us is at an end. Give me that sack and the English New Testament therein, with your slanderous book against the Eucharist. We are taking them away to be burned, and your hopes with them."

Wycliffe looked around the table, assessing the threats arrayed against him, but after one more peek out the window and seeing the figures were gone, he smiled and lifted the sack from the floor to the table, where the captain of the guard ensnared it before looking inside.

"Captain, bring that chaff with us so we might burn it publicly at Lambeth," said the archbishop, pushing off against the table and standing erect.

Wycliffe could not hold back a smile as the captain stammered, "Begging your pardon, Your Grace, but I don't think that's a wise idea given what's in here."

Sudbury lurched, grabbing the sack and pulling out the book from inside. There in his hand was a well-worn copy of the Latin Bible. Nothing else.

"Guards!" Archbishop Sudbury bawled. "Go to the church and find the ... the ..." He never finished the sentence. Enraged, he shoved his chaplains and the guards out of the Sparrow and the Stallion. "Where have the books gone?" he screamed into the night air.

Wycliffe remained at his table, tracing his fingers on the moist outline of his ale mug as he looked into the darkness. The Lollards had slipped away as planned. The English New Testaments and the other books that Sudbury thought he had snared were instead with them en route all over England. He tendered a prayer to his Saviour, "Keep them safe, Lord. May they proclaim Your truth. May they preach Your Word faithfully."

In a time of deep unrest and English rebellion against the strain of the Roman church, **JOHN WYCLIFFE** searched the Scriptures for the light of truth by which the Church could live. Upholding the ultimate authority of the Bible and the simplicity of the Church as God's people,

Wycliffe rejected the authority of popes and the doctrine of transubstantiation in Holy Communion. Perhaps his lasting legacy was his desire to have Scripture translated in the language of the English people, which he did from the Latin Vulgate. Although he died suddenly in 1384, many of his beliefs led future churchmen to call Wycliffe the "Morning Star of the Reformation".

UK

LUTTERWORTH

LONDON

JULIAN OF NORWICH

1398, Carrow Abbey, England

The gently falling rain sounded like whispers moving over the ground outside. The woman carefully completed her written thoughts in her elegant script before placing her quill on the table. Rubbing her hands slowly, she mused that of course she should have expected the rain. Her hands began to tire and ache whenever a shower or storm came in from the North Sea, and they were aching now. Smiling, and telling herself that rest was just as worthy an endeavor as work, Julian bowed her head and silently gave thanks to God for revealing His truth to her.

Any visitor to this bare room, this cell, would wonder how this fifty-five-year-old woman could find joy within the walls. But Julian never questioned the workings of God. She had committed her life to Him, and that was enough. As an anchoress, this room was where she lived in seclusion, praying, writing, and worshiping. This was the path on which her Savior had set her.

Seclusion, though, still allowed for some visitors. Servants brought her the food and drink she required. The prioress was kind enough to visit on occasion and bring writing materials for Julian's expanding volume. But she would not leave this cell. She was happy here, in this solitary room attached to the church. This was where God had blessed her so that she could be a blessing to the world.

A rumble of thunder caused Julian to raise her eyebrows; the storm was increasing in intensity. Rubbing her hands once more, she considered returning to her writing when she heard a series of patters in the wet churchyard. Even without looking, Julian could sense this was no haphazard movement of a stray animal; these were purposeful, if desperate, steps. And they were coming nearer.

And then came a knock on her door.

Julian peered into the darkness and outer gloom. She expected to see either the prioress or a servant bringing needed materials. She did not expect this visitor.

"Anchoress?" came the timid address from the shaking form outside the door.

Julian looked more closely. "Susanna!" she declared with equal parts joy and surprise. "What are you doing here? You are not one of my designated visitors!"

Susanna shifted her feet nervously, her eyes dropping. "I know, anchoress. I beg your pardon, and I have no right to expect an audience with you, except I have no one else to whom I might turn."

Julian gave a quizzical look. "No one in the abbey? No one in the church?"

Susanna sighed. "I can't say that I approached anyone in the abbey. But my heart is so vexed and battered. My spirit compelled me to come here, anchoress. I cannot explain why. I have a heavy burden, and I need one who can lift it from my soul."

Julian looked closely and saw tears flowing from Susanna's eyes. A whisper passed through Julian's heart. *Listen to her pain.*

Giving a slight smile, Julian whispered to Susanna. "Come closer my child. Perhaps God has brought you here for a reason."

For several minutes, there was a companionable silence, as the older anchoress seated on her bed and the younger nun on a chair outside the cell. Julian was content to let time pass until Susanna was comfortable enough to speak forth, and when she finally did, it was in the form of an apology.

"I am sorry for this intrusion," she began, "but in spite of the fact I am in this spiritual community, I am not confident any in the abbey would truly understand my affliction."

"No matter who fails to understand, my child," Julian replied, "God truly does." She paused, folding her hands together. "Tell me what vexes you."

Susanna choked on her first attempt, then steadied herself and slowly forced out the words. "I believe that God does not and cannot love me. I am so sinful that I must be outside of His affections."

Julian cocked her head to the side, but she was careful to smile warmly upon her visitor. "That may seem to others to be a serious charge against Almighty God," she said, "but to me it appears you have given much serious thought. Is this true?"

Susanna sniffled, tears splashing from her eyes to the stone floor, and she nodded.

"Well, then," Julian said slowly and carefully, "whatever you might believe about God in this moment, you have at least come here after careful reflection. But why me? Why now?"

Susanna wiped her eyes and rubbed the residue on her cloak. "I had heard that you were an authority on God's love, that you were writing a great deal about it. My heart is so troubled I believed coming to you was my only chance of comfort."

"That I was writing about it?"

Susanna nodded.

"Ah," Julian chuckled lightly, "the prioress Edith is most generous with providing material for my writing, but she can't help but tell others of what I am doing."

"I am truly sorry, anchoress," Susanna interrupted. "I did not mean to betray her."

"You have done no such thing, dear Susanna," Julian assured her, "but perhaps you can enlighten me why you believe God does not and cannot love you? What makes you say that?"

"Oh, anchoress," Susanna groaned, "how can God look upon us, upon me, without seeing the depths of my sin, both open rebellion and secret thoughts? How can a God so pure look upon someone so unlovely with His affection?"

Julian closed her eyes and breathed in and out, slowly. "Yes, yes," she finally responded, "that is a very natural question to ask. But do you mind if I answer your question with another question?"

"My question with one of your own?" Susanna asked.

"I believe," Julian said thoughtfully, "that questions provide a most illuminating opportunity to learn. Yes, my question would be this: Where is God to find the lovable, sinless people who are worthy of His love?"

Susanna paused. "I don't understand."

"Well," Julian continued, "God does not do His work in isolated fashion, does He? From what you know of the Scriptures, isn't He constantly working through and speaking to others?"

"Yes," Susanna admitted, "there is that."

"God constantly inhabits the lives of others, knows us, and desires to be known by us. Now answer me this: Can you think of anyone who avoids sin completely? Ever?"

"No, anchoress," Susanna confessed, "I can't say I do."

"So if there is sin in everyone, there is something unlovable within us all, correct?"

Susanna frowned. "Your teaching makes sense, but I am not sure how comforting it is."

"But don't you see, dear Susanna," Julian replied, "that sinful people are the only creatures God has at His disposal! Whom else shall He love except the unworthy?"

Susanna nodded slowly. "So I am not uniquely sinful or unlovable?"

"Susanna, I believe you are noble for looking in your heart and seeing your sin. We should all seek to be so watchful. But this can come at a price. I think what you have been doing is seeing your own unworthiness—true as that may be for all of us—and forgetting about the merciful God Himself."

When Susanna didn't respond, Julian continued. "Maybe this might help. Now understand that I have not been outside my cell in ages, so what I am saying I do from memory of my knowledge of the area of Norwich. Did you grow up in this area?"

"I did."

"You did occasionally, before you entered the abbey, walk near the River Wensum?"

"Yes, I did. There is a lovely bend in the river near Thorpe Wood where I loved to spend time years ago."

"Ah, yes. Well, as I said, so much of this is from memory, but as you walked by the Wensum, was the level of the water always the same?"

"I suppose not," Susanna admitted. "At times, the Wensum was high, nearly over its banks, and at times it was quite low. Depending on the time of day, it could be high or low tide."

"Indeed," Julian agreed. "Now permit me to make a comparison. I think you have a view of God that His love for you could change, like the Wensum tides."

"I suppose I do," Susanna conceded.

"I think that might be a natural thing, but I think the tides are more like our perspective. Sometimes we feel lovable, sometimes we don't. Just yesterday, Susanna, I wrote a number of pages about God and had a glorious time of prayer. It would be a simple thing for me to feel more loved by God because I experienced a closeness to Him through my writing and prayer. But the week before, I remember I had a day when I was very frustrated. I had not slept well the night before. My prayers wandered everywhere in an unfocused fashion. I didn't sense a particular closeness to God that day. That is what I mean about the Wensum tides. They are up and down, and so are we as we sense closeness to and affection from God, but that does not mean that God loves us any less, nor has He abandoned us. Remember what our Lord said to Joshua before he led the Hebrews into Canaan? I will never leave you nor forsake you. Whether we sense that or not, it makes no difference to God. He continues to uphold us and love us. And His love includes you, Susanna!"

"That does seem entirely too good to be true, anchoress," said Susanna. "But I would hope it is true."

"Dearest Susanna," Julian replied, "let me tell you of another experience which I believe might be helpful. I really think that many people believe that when hardship enters their life, it is evidence of God's displeasure."

"That seems natural to assume," said Susanna, hedging. "Although perhaps you are going to tell me that this natural assumption is not always a correct one?"

Julian smiled. "You are learning quickly, dear one. Yes, there was a day, twenty-five years ago to be precise, when what I endured took me further into the love of God rather than away from it."

Julian stood from her bed, clasping her hands in front of her. "When I was thirty years old, a devastating sickness swept through Norwich. This was before I began living within this cell, so when I fell gravely ill, I was placed in a house elsewhere in the city. I pleaded that God would, in His grace, restore me to health, but the more I prayed, the more feverish I became. Finally, a priest came to pray over me because he was certain I was at the door of death. For that matter, I was certain of death myself."

"Were you afraid?" Susanna asked.

"In truth, I had no time to consider whether I was or not," Julian recalled. "As the priest prayed over me and offered me to God's care, I suddenly had an experience that left me shaken. Whether it was a dream or a vision I don't know, but I do remember seeing Jesus Himself, dying on the cross in horrific agony. I remember thinking what love He must have felt for His followers that He would be willing to die for us, for me!"

Julian sat back on the bed and unclasped her hands. "Over the next few days, that sight returned to me and was accompanied by another miracle: My fever left me and I was restored to health! I would never say that the experience of coming so close to death was wonderful, but the remembrance of the love of Jesus for me, His child, was more than worth my endurance of that trial."

Susanna grew quiet. Her misgivings about God's love were passing away in the face of what Julian had shared with her. "Then how may I live knowing this always? It is one thing to hear this in your cell, but I'll have to leave you eventually and return to my daily life. How do I go on trusting in the love of God moment by moment?"

"By remembering your hope is not in what you have done, my child," Julian exulted, the glow of her smile giving light to the room. "For it is within that royal, happy friendship of your gentle Lord Jesus that He holds on to you and will never abandon you, no matter your sin. Yes, there is much that threatens to cover us in death, sweet child, but the touch of God is the soft light of His mercy and grace. He is not displeased with you, Susanna! He has brought you here today to show you His love!"

The tears were flowing unbidden from Susanna's eyes as Julian continued, taking Susanna's hands in her own. "Your failing, your sin," whispered Julian, "shall not stop Him from loving you. For His peace works in you, His love finds its way deep within you, even if you do not always sense His peace or His love. And He suffered for you, Susanna. Why? Let me whisper it to you."

Susanna could hold back no more, weeping openly as she knelt at Julian's feet as the anchoress continued. "Love, child. The love of God. Why? To show you are His dearly beloved. So that even if you do not understand your pain, you will know He loves you. He holds on to you, my child; He loves you. And why? Because He simply wants to love you. May Jesus grant you this always, dearest Susanna. Amen, in His name."

Although **JULIAN** never left her cell as an anchoress in Norwich, England, she made a powerful impact on others through her writings and convictions of God's undying and powerful love. Her *Revelations of Divine Love* remains a devotional classic, and the book is the first book written in English by a woman. Her recollections of her visions and encounters with Christ had a powerful impact on her followers, and her sweetness of spirit and compassion toward others endeared her to many. Although this story is fictional, it is highly representative of the gentle love and wise counsel Julian would offer anyone in need of the comfort of Christ.

JOHN HUS

July 1415, Constance, Holy Roman Empire

Normally, John Hus[1] thought, one would go to a library to read and study. But, now he often went to the library to witness the debates. A number of scholars from Bohemia had traveled to England for study; the fact that King Richard II of England had married Anne, the sister of Bohemia's king, had made relations and student exchanges between the two lands much easier. His friends had recently returned from Oxford and excitedly reported about the turmoil there in the name of truth, and Hus intended to discover what they have learned.

"What indeed are you talking about, men?" he would ask them.

"It is like a torrent has been unleashed there," exclaimed one, "because this John Wycliffe opened so many eyes while he lived to what the Church has hidden from its people."

"Hidden?" Hus asked. "But how?"

"What else can we expect when the Church is so divided against itself now?" the other laughed bitterly. "The present schism is a foolish joke! The French demand their own pope, the Italians the same. Why should we believe the papacy has any power when nations seem to manage well enough without it, especially given the poor run of popes we've had lately?"

"The time has come for us to assert our religious liberties as Wycliffe has done in England," the first added.

1. Jan Hus' name is also written as Jan Huss in English, but is Jan Hus when written in Czech.

"The people should be able to hear and read the Word of God in their own language, all of which should be at the heart of Christian worship."

"The Scriptures over the sacraments?" Hus was surprised. "Are you certain of what you're asking for? The Church is sure to respond swiftly against this."

"But that is precisely why we should be raising such questions," the other urged him. "Look at the corruption within the walls of the Church even today. Bishops take bribes and, for a princely sum, they are willing to induct priests in some very affluent parishes, with no regard for the priest's morality or holy conduct! Are you saying these are legitimate maneuvers?"

Hus had to agree. "No. It is heavy with the spirit of Simon the sorcerer, begging Peter to sell him the power of the Holy Spirit. Many seek power in Christ's Church through bribes and negotiation."

"Including your priest at home, John," the first one reminded him. "Promoted by your bishop for a price of a full years' wages! You can't possibly think such a man is worthy of respect, or of administering the sacraments." He leaned on the table and stared directly at Hus. "At some point you must stand firmly, even if you stand alone!"

Hus thought back to that statement later in 1410 as he entered the church in Prague. The crowds that had gathered at Bethlehem Chapel that day huddled in the cold interior of the church as Hus ascended to the pulpit. How dearly these beloved souls need assurance. How deeply they require comfort as the storm clouds are about to break, and I don't know if I shall survive this tempest.

He opened his Bible and began, his ears pricking up and taking in the shouts approaching the church. "I wish to remind you today," he told the congregation, "that in the midst of life and death, we can have full faith and confidence in the shed blood of Jesus Christ. The apostle Paul himself reminds us that he resolved to know nothing .... nothing ... except Jesus Christ and Him crucified. To that hope we pledge ourselves this day and forevermore."

He paused, taking in the hopeful yet worried looks on the faces of the worshipers. "I must solemnly warn all of you dear ones that today is a day that we have feared might come. The authorities have come forth to declare me excommunicated from the Church of Rome and to close our place of worship." He allowed the news to sink in and the frantic cries of the assembly to subside, then waved his hand about. "I say do not fear! Like the early church, we may face persecution, but if they close this chapel and scatter us, even more churches will arise. Though they declare us enemies of Rome, we shall be Bohemian people and shall establish rays of Gospel light throughout our land." He stopped, sensing fully the gravity of this moment. "And if they take us and burn us alive, it shall serve as a beacon of salvation to our land and to lands beyond."

He said no more, wondering if he had just uttered a self-fulfilling prophecy.

The day of fulfillment would come a few years later in the great city of Constance.

With a mighty heave, the prison guard pulled on the gate and swung it open, the iron rails scraping over the stone floor of the cell. Looking into the flickering candlelight, he located the prisoner, bearded and gaunt, on the stool in the corner. "You, Hus!" he barked. "They have called for you again in the cathedral! Let's get going!" He stood defiantly and waggled the chains in his hand, reminding the prisoner to step forward to be shackled at the wrists.

Wearily, John Hus pushed off his chair, his mouth parched and his legs unsteady. The food had been abominable the previous night. No change there, for every meal had been the same during his six-month captivity in this vile cell. Never was it washed, rarely was he given clean clothes or fresh food, and the driftless interior of the jail chamber granted him no fresh air. All of these realities conspired to make him ill with constant headaches and occasional vomiting. He had been accosted by a fever over the past five days which refused to leave him, and every measure of his strength was sapped. Just last year, the muscles on his stocky frame stuck out like heavy cords; now his skin hung loosely over his arms as his mocking captor made sure the chains were tight.

"This way," the guard snarled, and the two of them headed down the musty corridor.

"At some point you must stand firmly, even if you stand alone!" The words entered Hus' mind again.

"The prisoner will answer the question!"

Hus snapped out of his reverie and found himself in the nave of the cathedral. The six hundred souls arrayed against Hus were murmuring loudly at the sight of his distraction, and their complaints loudly filled the cathedral. Hus looked to his right, where Emperor Sigismund sat preening, his very body language demanding Hus give a response immediately.

"I am sorry for my delay," Hus finally replied, "but I will gladly recant my position on any accusation against me as long as my prosecutors will direct all here to where I am proved wrong by Holy Scripture."

"Do not play with words, you heretic!" The words exploded from the mouth of the bishop. "We are no prosecutors, but your fathers in the faith, charged by God Almighty with the salvation of your soul. We stand ready to welcome your return to the family of Christ. You seek only the danger of wandering into the dangerous cliffs of heresy!"

"And as I said, I shall gratefully accept that if you reveal it from Scripture!" Hus replied calmly but firmly.

"First of all, the Church has taught we receive the grace of Christ through the use of indulgences. You have denied that!" You deny the comfort that men can have from these gifts that might lessen their time outside the gates of St. Peter in heaven," the bishop stated.

"A true denial," Hus answered plainly, "and as you cannot and will not respond with Scripture, you reveal that you speak with no true defense for your actions! And as to denying comfort, I will always deny men comfort when it is based on false hope. When that false hope denies the overflowing love of God in His Son that saves His precious people!"

"You savage beast!" howled Carlo Malatesta. The prince of Rimini scowled at the stooped and dirty Hus. "Your entire ministry in Prague has been nothing but a full-armed assault against the glory of the Church and its leaders, the family that tastes of Christ's Body and Blood in the Mass, which you decry!"

"Not so," Hus snapped. "I have not attacked anything of the Supper of our Lord. But you are correct if you mean I wish to clearly show who is the Church. You say it is all the faithful followers of Rome. I say the flock of the Good Shepherd is His sheep throughout all ages, joined to Him in simple trust in His death and resurrection alone, and He will rescue them from the wrath to come!"

"Not so," replied the bishop, as Hus saw Emperor Sigismund squirm in his throne. "If you speak thus, then you are in fact saying that includes those who live outside the authority of the Pope himself!"

"Because the Pope is not the head of the Church!" Hus grunted loudly. "Only Jesus Christ has dominion and glory in the Church and throughout all ages! The Pope—whoever he might be—is neither perfectly authoritative, nor infallible, nor supreme. Even our Eastern Orthodox fellow believers should be given some credit in this; they have conducted their faith for years without the oversight of any pope!"

"You are out of ..."

"And speaking of which," Hus interposed himself, "if the Pope is supreme and the representative of Christ on earth, then why is this council having to decide which of the three of them is the legitimate one?"

"And what do you expect? Who else should intervene?"

"Is it really incumbent upon us to obey immoral priests and bishops?" asked Hus. "If the Church cannot bring itself to its knees in repentance and reform, then why should those who reign from the thrones of nations buckle their knees for them!"

"Outrage!" screamed several in the assembly.

"Blasphemy!" roared more from the back.

"Not blasphemy," Hus retorted, his lungs feeling as though they would burst. "Because the very heartbeat of service to Christ is at stake. Even if those hands which pass on the sacrament of the Body and Blood of our Lord be filthy, their mouths must be clean when they proclaim the riches of Scripture, which stands above the Mass as the height of ministry to Christ's sheep!"

"Devil scum!" came the hiss from the emperor's throne. Hus turned and saw Sigismund, scepter in a hand that clamped upon it viciously. Shaking his head amidst the tumult in the cathedral, Hus gave the emperor a peaceful yet sad look.

Even you, he thought. *My fate is sealed. So be it.*

Rough hands seized Hus and dragged him to the front. His arms ached from the guard's grip and his body moaned from lack of food and drink. He tottered in front of the legates. Lord Christ, I have tried to be faithful to you in my little life, he prayed silently. Help me to be faithful in what I sense will be my death. A number of men in bishop's vestments surrounded Hus in a semicircle behind him. Craning his neck, Hus counted six of them.

"John Hus," the bishop began, "in spite of our tender attempts to bring you back into the fold of the Lord's sheep pen, we cannot abide by your wanton false teaching and your hatred for the Church of Christ. We hereby condemn you for your heresies which you stubbornly refuse to retract! And to underscore the severity of your actions, we strip you of your priestly title and standing!"

At that moment, the six bishops, jeering and taunting and joined in by the crowd within the cathedral, set upon Hus with vigor. One produced some shears and began clipping away at Hus' hair as the cheers grew louder. Ripping at his clothes the clerics reduced Hus to a sallow-skinned, shivering image of skin and bones within a linen undergarment. One of them stepped forward and shoved a paper hat on Hus' head, eliciting roars of laughter from the congregation.

"Hah, hah!" cackled another. "If you could only see, you foolish dunce! Red devils prancing about your skull and you bowing before Satan himself. 'Oh, please take me, my lord and master!' Well, you'll see the prince of darkness soon enough!"

"If I do," Hus said quietly, "I'd recognize his face as yours, sadly."

The bishop's foot bisected Hus's rib cage with staggering force. Hus fell to the floor, coughing blood, and got to his knees with great difficulty. Sigismund ordered him pulled roughly to his feet. "Now you shall see who holds the power around here, heretic," the emperor roared.

"The fact that you say that," Hus wept sadly, "shows you do not acknowledge who rules this world."

The straw was at least clean, Hus thought as he looked at the site of his imminent death. It would offer a different place than his prison cell that had been his home for the last six months. He felt the guards tying his hands behind his back and securing them to the stake. He saw the executioner draw near with a bucket and dauber of oil at one side and a lit torch in his hand.

This is the end, Lord, Hus prayed. And as always, you are faithful to me.

"John Hus," came the voice of the imperial marshal, "are you even now willing to recant your vile heresies and place yourself under the mercy of God?"

Hus looked at him, at the executioner, at Emperor Sigismund, and the crowd expanding beyond in multiple rows in the city square. "No," he said, bending his knees as well as he could to approximate a kneeling position. "I pray that God would forgive all of you who position yourselves as my enemies. And while I will not recant, I commit, as always, my soul to my most gracious Lord Jesus Christ, who loved me and gave Himself for me. For the same truth of the Gospel which I have written, taught, and preached, as the faithful of history have done, I am ready to lay down my life and die with joy today."

"How can you die with joy?" sneered the emperor, as the executioner lit the straw. "All you are is a goose to be roasted."

"Because I die today, yet truth shall live," Hus rasped as the straw crackled with the heat. "And today you can burn the goose, but years from now a swan will come, and you will be incapable of killing him!"

The flames rose slowly, the smell of the blaze and straw melding together into a gradual burn. As the fire grew, John Hus looked toward the heavens, thinking of his beloved band of Christians back in Bohemia, now as ever under the sovereign mercy of Christ. The fire began to roar around him, its tongues pricking his exposed skin as he uttered one final prayer from his parched mouth.

"Jesus Christ, Son of the living God, have mercy on us."

JOHN HUS (1372-1415) came under the influence of John Wycliffe's teaching while at the University of Prague, where he later served as a professor and dean. His firm Scriptural teaching unleashed a passion for the Gospel in Prague and throughout the land of Bohemia. This Hussite Church that grew from his teaching became the dominant religious body in that area in spite of much persecution. This church eventually forced the papacy to accept its existence and then embraced the Protestant faith in the sixteenth century forging a national church movement. Speaking out against the abuses of the Catholic Church and proclaiming the absolute authority of Scripture, Hus ministered at Bethlehem Chapel in Prague until it was closed and he was denounced as a heretic. In spite of Emperor Sigismund's promise of safe conduct at the Council of Constance, Hus was thrown into prison, mistreated, tried, and sentenced to death. His martyrdom increased the spirit of unrest against the corruption of the Church and helped pave the way for the dawn of the Protestant Reformation.

WHERE WE GET OUR INFORMATION

Bernard of Clairvaux. On Loving God. Public domain material at Christian Classics Ethereal Library at Calvin College. https://www.ccel.org/ccel/bernard/loving_god.toc.html

Chesterton, G.K. Saint Francis of Assisi. New York, NY: Image Books, rev. 1990.

Copleston, Frederick. A History of Philosophy, Volume II: Medieval Philosophy. New York, NY: Image Books, 1962.

Crowley, Roger. 1453: The Holy War for Constantinople and the Clash of Islam and the West. New York, NY: Hyperion Books, 2005.

D'Aguiliers, Raymond. The Conquest of Jerusalem. At https://christianhistoryinstitute.org/study/module/crusaders

Durant, Will. The Story of Civilization: The Age of Faith. New York, NY: Simon & Schuster, 1950.

Fremantle, Anne. The Age of Belief: The Medieval Philosophers. New York, NY: Mentor Books, 1954.

Gonzalez, Justo L. The Story of Christianity, Volume 1: The Early Church to the Dawn of the Reformation. New York, NY: Harper & Row, 1984.

Jones, Dan. Magna Carta: The Birth of Liberty. New York, NY: Viking, 2015.

Lacey, Robert. Great Tales From English History: The Truth About King Arthur, Lady Godiva, Richard the Lionheart, and More. New York, NY: Little, Brown, and Co., 2003.

Leeming, J.R. Stephen Langton, Hero of Magna Charta. CreateSpace, 2015.

McCann, Abbot Justin. Saint Benedict: The Story of the Man and His Work, rev. ed. Garden City, NY: Image Books, 1958.

McGrath, Alister, ed. The Christian Theology Reader, Third Edition. Hoboken, NJ: Wiley-Blackwell, 2006.

Needham, Nick. 2000 Years of Christ's Power: Volume 2: The Middle Ages. Ross-shire, UK: Christian Focus Publications, 2016.

Noble, Thomas F.X. and Julia M.H. Smith, eds. The Cambridge History of Christianity, Volume 3: Early Medieval Christianities, © 600-1100. Cambridge, UK: Cambridge University Press, 2008.

Noll, Mark. Turning Points: Decisive Moments in the History of Christianity. Grand Rapids, MI: Baker Academic, 2001.

Olson, Roger. The Story of Christian Theology: Twenty Centuries of Tradition and Reform. Downers Grove, IL: IVP Academic, 1999.

Riche, Pierre. Daily Life in the World of Charlemagne. Philadelphia, PA: University of Pennsylvania Press, 1978.

Ritchie, Bruce. Columba: The Faith of an Island Soldier. Ross-shire, UK: Christian Focus Publications, 2019.

Rubin, Miri and Walter Simons, eds. The Cambridge History of Christianity, Volume 4: Christianity in Western Europe, © 1100-1500. Cambridge, UK: Cambridge University Press, 2009.

Schaff, Philip, ed. The Nicene and Post-Nicene Fathers: Volume XIII, Second Series. Grand Rapids, MI: Eerdmans, 1956.

Shelley, Bruce. Church History in Plain Language. Nashville, TN: Thomas Nelson, 1995.

Thomas Aquinas. The Summa Theologica, rev. Daniel J. Sullivan. Chicago, IL: Britannica Great Books, 1952.

Walton, Robert C. Chronological and Background Charts of Church History. Grand Rapids, MI: Zondervan, 1986.

Wedeck, Harry E., ed. Putnam's Dark and Middle Ages Reader. New York, NY: Capricorn Books, 1965.

Woodbridge, John D., ed. Great Leaders of the Christian Church. Chicago, IL: Moody Press, 1988.

Redemption

The Church in Ancient Times

Luke H. Davis

- Part of new 'Risen Hope' church history series
- Covers 3 BC to 476 AD
- For teens

The story of the ancient Church is one of a people who were finding their way over many years by the light that God shined forth for them. Today, we are looking back over the centuries with many more years of understanding but we stand on the shoulders of those who braved persecution, death, debate, and mystery on behalf of generations to come. From the Apostle Peter at Pentecost in Jerusalem to St. Patrick on the shores of Ireland in the year 432 – the ancient church has much to teach the church of today.

ISBN: 978-1-5271-0800-4

Christian Focus Publications publishes books for adults and children under its four main imprints: Christian Focus, CF4K, Mentor and Christian Heritage. Our books reflect our conviction that God's Word is reliable and Jesus is the way to know him, and live for ever with him.

Our children's publication list covers pre-school to early teens. We also publish personal and family devotional titles, biographies and inspirational stories that children will love.

From pre-school board books to teenage apologetics, we have it covered!

Christian Focus Publications Ltd,
Geanies House, Fearn, Ross-shire,
IV20 1TW, Scotland,
United Kingdom.

Find us at our web page:
www.christianfocus.com